488 Bacardi Rum Base Cocktails

Lev Well

ISBN: 1518878199
ISBN-13: 978-1518878190

Disclaimer

All recipes are used at the discretion of the consumer. We cannot be responsible for any hazards, loss or damage that may occur as a result of any recipe used.
For those with special needs, allergies, requirements or health problems, in the event of any doubt, please contact your medical adviser prior to the use of any recipe.

CONTENTS

5

100 Miles per Hour recipe

Description

A delicious recipe for 100 Miles per Hour, with Wild Turkey® bourbon whiskey, Bacardi® 151 rum, Southern Comfort® peach liqueur, Yukon Jack® Canadian whisky, grenadine syrup and Blue Curacao liqueur. Also lists similar drin

Ingredients

1/2 oz Wild Turkey® bourbon whiskey
1/2 oz Bacardi® 151 rum
1/2 oz Southern Comfort® peach liqueur
1/2 oz Yukon Jack® Canadian whisky
1/2 oz grenadine syrup
2 oz Blue Curacao liqueur

Instructions

Mix all ingredients together over ice in a highball glass. Shake up, then top with sprite and serve.

Serving

Highball Glass
****

12 Gauge Shottie recipe

Description

A delicious recipe for 12 Gauge Shottie, with Corona® lager and Bacardi® Limon rum.

Ingredients

1 bottle Corona® lager
1/8 bottle Bacardi® Limon rum

Instructions

Drink the Corona lager down to the neck (where the bottle curves inwards). Fill up the neck with Bacardi Limon rum. Put your finger over the bottle and shake. Enjoy.

Serving

Beer Mug
****

20/20 Lemon recipe

Description

A delicious recipe for 20/20 Lemon, with Mad Dog® grape wine and Bacardi® Limon rum.

Ingredients

3/4 cup Mad Dog® grape wine

1/4 cup Bacardi® Limon rum

Instructions

Pour MD 20/20 (try any flavor) into a cup. Add Bacardi limon rum, and serve.

Serving

Cup
****

252 recipe

Description

A delicious recipe for 252, with Bacardi® 151 rum and Wild Turkey® bourbon whiskey.

Ingredients

1/2 oz Bacardi® 151 rum
1/2 oz Wild Turkey® bourbon whiskey

Instructions

Pour both ingredients into a shot glass in equal parts, and serve.

Serving

Shot Glass
****

302 recipe

Description

A delicious recipe for 302, with Bacardi® 151 rum, Everclear® alcohol and Dr. Pepper® soda.

Ingredients

1/2 oz Bacardi® 151 rum
1/2 oz Everclear® alcohol
2 oz Dr. Pepper® soda

Instructions

Shake all ingredients briefly together in a highball glass, and serve.

Serving

Highball Glass
****

357 Magnum recipe

Description

A delicious recipe for 357 Magnum, with Bacardi® 151 rum, vodka, amaretto almond liqueur and 7-Up®

soda.

Ingredients

1 oz Bacardi® 151 rum
1 oz vodka
2 oz amaretto almond liqueur
2 1/2 oz 7-Up® soda

Instructions

Pour the Bacardi 151 rum into a highball glass filled with ice cubes. Add the vodka and amaretto. Fill with 7-up, and serve.

Serving

Highball Glass
****

414SS Daiquiri recipe

Description

A delicious recipe for 414SS Daiquiri, with Bacardi® 151 rum, Bacardi® light rum and daiquiri mix.

Ingredients

1 1/2 cups Bacardi® 151 rum
1 cup Bacardi® light rum
1 package daiquiri mix

Instructions

Add daiquiri mix and the required amount of ice stated on the packet to a blender. Add the Bacardi light rum and then the Bacardi 151. Splash in some more 151 if desired. Blend together for a few seconds, and pour into cocktail glasses. Attempt to drink.

Serving

Cocktail Glass
****

A Clockwork Tangerine recipe

Description

A delicious recipe for A Clockwork Tangerine, with Sprite® soda, Kool-Aid® Tangerine mix, Bacardi® gold rum and Smirnoff® vodka.

Ingredients

12 oz Sprite® soda
1 packet Kool-Aid® Tangerine mix
1 oz Bacardi® gold rum
1 oz Smirnoff® vodka

Instructions

Combine all ingredients in a beef pilsner. Stir together, and serve.

Serving

Beer Pilsner
****

Acapulco Twister recipe

Description

A delicious recipe for Acapulco Twister, with ice, lemons, salt, peppers, Tabasco® sauce, clamato juice, Bacardi® Limon rum and Corona® Extra lager.

Ingredients

ice
juice of 1 lemons
1 pinch salt
1 pinch peppers
3 drops Tabasco® sauce
1/2 oz clamato juice
1 1/2 oz Bacardi® Limon rum
4 oz Corona® Extra lager

Instructions

Mix the lemon, tabasco sauce, clamato juice, salt and pepper. Fill the glass with some ice, add the rum and fill with Corona beer.

Serving

Beer Mug
****

Acid Bomb recipe

Description

A delicious recipe for Acid Bomb, with Bacardi® Limon rum, Corona® Extra lager, lemon and salt.

Ingredients

2 - 3 oz Bacardi® Limon rum
1 bottle Corona® Extra lager
1 slice lemon
salt

Instructions

1. Crack open the bottle of Corona Extra and drop the lemon slice inside.

2. Serve a double-shot of Bacardi Limon with the rim of the shot glass layered with margarita salt.

3. Take the double-shot (holding the double shot in your mouth), and fill the rest of your mouth (with the double shot still inside) with Corona Extra.

4. Have a friend (with the mix of Bacardi and Corona in your mouth) shake your head for a solid 3 seconds, on the count of 3 down the mix in one swallow.

Serving
Bottle
****

Acid Rain recipe

Description
A delicious recipe for Acid Rain, with Snapple® Rain soda and Bacardi® Limon rum.

Ingredients
13 oz Snapple® Rain soda
7 oz Bacardi® Limon rum

Instructions
Drink about a third of the bottle of Snapple Rain, and then fill it back up with bacardi. Put the cap back on and shake it up.

****

ACID recipe

Description
A delicious recipe for ACID, with Bacardi® 151 rum, Wild Turkey® bourbon whiskey and Coca-Cola®.

Ingredients
1 oz Bacardi® 151 rum
1 oz Wild Turkey® bourbon whiskey
Coca-Cola®

Instructions
Poor in the 151 first followed by the 101 served with a Coke or Dr Pepper chaser.

Serving
Shot Glass
****

Acid Water recipe

Description

A delicious recipe for Acid Water, with Bacardi® 151 rum, moonshine whiskey, Everclear® alcohol and 7-Up® soda.

Ingredients

1 oz Bacardi® 151 rum
1 oz moonshine whiskey
1 oz Everclear® alcohol
1 oz 7-Up® soda

Instructions

Pour the Bacardi, Moonshine and Everclear into an old-fashioned or highball glass. Add the 7-up, stir briefly, and serve.

Serving

Highball Glass
****

Adam Bomb recipe

Description

A delicious recipe for Adam Bomb, with Jose Cuervo® Especial gold tequila, Absolut® vodka, Bacardi® white rum, triple sec, fruits, ice, sugar and fruit juice.

Ingredients

1 part Jose Cuervo® Especial gold tequila
1 part Absolut® vodka
1 part Bacardi® white rum
1/2 part triple sec
fruits
1/2 glass ice
sugar
2 pints fruit juice

Instructions

1. Add ice to a blender (or to a glass if you prefer on the rocks).

2. Add the fruit and fruit juice depending on personal preference, then add the rum, vodka, tequila, and triple sec. Blend until smooth.

3. Rim a glass with sugar or salt and pour in the mixture. Garnish with a lemon or lime slice.

Serving

Margarita Glass
****

After Work Special recipe

Description

A delicious recipe for After Work Special, with Amaretto Di Amore® liqueur, Malibu® coconut rum, Bacardi® white rum, orange juice and pineapple juice.

Ingredients

3 oz Amaretto Di Amore® liqueur
2 oz Malibu® coconut rum
1 oz Bacardi® white rum
3 - 6 oz orange juice
3 - 6 oz pineapple juice

Instructions

Pour the Di Amore amaretto, Malibu rum and Bacardi rum over 5 ice cubes in a hurricane glass. Fill the rest of the glass with orange juice and pineapple juice, to taste, and serve.

Serving

Hurricane Glass
****

Afterburner recipe

Description

A delicious recipe for Afterburner, with Aftershock® Hot & Cool cinnamon schnapps and Bacardi® 151 rum.

Ingredients

1/2 shot Aftershock® Hot & Cool cinnamon schnapps
1/2 shot Bacardi® 151 rum

Instructions

Pour both ingredients and let them mix somewhat. (You can stir it to help it out)

Serving

Shot Glass
****

Alaine Cocktail recipe

Description

A delicious recipe for Alaine Cocktail, with Bacardi® Limon rum, amaretto almond liqueur and cranberry juice.

Ingredients

1 oz Bacardi® Limon rum
1 oz amaretto almond liqueur
1 oz cranberry juice

Instructions

Combine the Bacardi Limon rum, amaretto and cranberry juice in a cocktail shaker half-filled with ice cubes. Shake, strain into a cocktail glass, and serve.

Serving

Cocktail Glass
****

Alebrije recipe

Description

A delicious recipe for Alebrije, with ice, grenadine syrup, Absolut® vodka, Bacardi® white rum, amaretto almond liqueur, gin, white tequila, orange juice and pineapple juice.

Ingredients

ice
1 splash grenadine syrup
1/2 oz Absolut® vodka
1/2 oz Bacardi® white rum
1/2 oz amaretto almond liqueur
1/2 oz gin
1/2 oz white tequila
2 oz orange juice
2 oz pineapple juice

Instructions

First mix some orange juice and pinapple juice in equal parts, and color it with some grenadine (as sweet as you want). This is "conga mix". Fill the glass with ice, add the five licours and mix them, fill the glass with some conga mix and enjoy.

Serving

Hurricane Glass
****

Amnesia recipe

Description

A delicious recipe for Amnesia, with DeKuyper Island Blue Pucker, DeKuyper® Watermelon Pucker schnapps, Bacardi® Limon rum, orange juice and pineapple juice.

Ingredients

1/2 oz DeKuyper Island Blue Pucker
1/2 oz DeKuyper® Watermelon Pucker schnapps
1/2 oz Bacardi® Limon rum
1/3 oz orange juice
3 splashes pineapple juice

Instructions

Combine both the watermelon and grape-flavored schnapps, Bacardi limon, orange juice and pineapple juice in an old-fashioned glass. Serve.

Serving

Old-Fashioned Glass
****

Angry Chameleon recipe

Description

A delicious recipe for Angry Chameleon, with Kool-Aid® Cherry mix, Bacardi® white rum and Mountain Dew® citrus soda.

Ingredients

2 tsp Kool-Aid® Cherry mix
2 oz Bacardi® white rum
6 oz Mountain Dew® citrus soda

Instructions

Dissolve kool-aid mixture in rum, add mountain dew, and serve.

Serving

Collins Glass
****

Anjorska recipe

Description

A delicious recipe for Anjorska, with Bacardi® Limon rum, Passoa® liqueur, sweet and sour mix, cranberry juice and grape juice.

Ingredients

1 1/3 oz Bacardi® Limon rum
2/3 oz Passoa® liqueur
1 2/3 oz sweet and sour mix
1 2/3 oz cranberry juice
2/3 oz grape juice

Instructions

Pour the Bacardi, Passoa, sweet and sour mix, and juices into a highball glass almost filled with ice cubes. Stir well, garnish with a slice of lime, and serve.

Serving

Highball Glass
****

Ann Sheridan Cocktail recipe

Description

A delicious recipe for Ann Sheridan Cocktail, with Bacardi® white rum, Orange Curacao liqueur and lime juice.

Ingredients

2/3 oz Bacardi® white rum
1/3 oz Orange Curacao liqueur
3/4 oz lime juice

Instructions

Pour the Bacardi rum, orange curacao and lime juice into a cocktail shaker half-filled with ice cubes. Shake well, and strain into a cocktail glass. Garnish with a lime wedge, and serve.

Serving

Cocktail Glass
****

Anti-Freeze #4 recipe

Description

A delicious recipe for Anti-Freeze #4, with vodka, Blue Curacao liqueur, Bacardi® 151 rum and peppermint schnapps.

Ingredients

1/2 oz vodka
1/2 oz Blue Curacao liqueur
1/2 oz Bacardi® 151 rum
1/2 oz peppermint schnapps

Instructions

Chill w/ ice cubes in shaker. Pour into rocks glass or split into two shots.

Serving

Old-Fashioned Glass
****

Apple 151 recipe

Description

A delicious recipe for Apple 151, with apple juice and Bacardi® 151 rum.

Ingredients

2 oz apple juice
1 oz Bacardi® 151 rum

Instructions

Stir ingredients together in a mug with ice, and serve.

Serving

Beer Mug
****

Apple Mojito recipe

Description

A delicious recipe for Apple Mojito, with Bacardi® Big Apple rum, club soda, lime, sugar and mint.

Ingredients

2 oz Bacardi® Big Apple rum
6 oz club soda
3 lime wedges
2 tsp sugar
3 fresh mint sprigs

Instructions

Add the lime, sugar and mint sprigs to a highball glass and muddle with a muddler. Add several ice cubes and pour in the Bacardi apple rum. Top with club soda (adjust to taste), and stir. Garnish with an apple slice and a lime wedge, and serve.

Serving

Highball Glass
****

Arizona Aztec recipe

Description

A delicious recipe for Arizona Aztec, with Jose Cuervo® Especial gold tequila, Bacardi® Limon rum, Captain Morgan® Original spiced rum and Coca-Cola®.

Ingredients

1 3/4 oz Jose Cuervo® Especial gold tequila
1 3/4 oz Bacardi® Limon rum
1 3/4 oz Captain Morgan® Original spiced rum
6 3/4 oz Coca-Cola®

Instructions

Pour the Jose Cuervo gold tequila, Bacardi Limon rum and Captain Morgan spiced rum into a highball glass. Stir well. Fill with Coca-cola, stir again, and serve.

Serving

Highball Glass

****

Army Ranger recipe

Description

A delicious recipe for Army Ranger, with Bacardi® 151 rum, Red Bull® energy drink and Jagermeister® herbal liqueur.

Ingredients

1/2 oz Bacardi® 151 rum
8 oz can Red Bull® energy drink
1 oz Jagermeister® herbal liqueur

Instructions

Mix the Jagermeister herbal liqueur, Bacardi 151 rum and Red Bull energy drink in a mug or tall glass. Float a slice of both lime and lemon on top, and serve.

Serving

Mug
****

Asia 9.0 recipe

Description

A delicious recipe for Asia 9.0, with Bacardi® 151 rum, Southern Comfort® peach liqueur, Midori® melon liqueur, amaretto almond liqueur and pineapple juice.

Ingredients

1 1/2 oz Bacardi® 151 rum
1 1/2 oz Southern Comfort® peach liqueur
1 1/2 oz Midori® melon liqueur
1 1/2 oz amaretto almond liqueur
6 oz can pineapple juice

Instructions

Combine all ingredients together in a cocktail shaker half-filled with ice cubes. Shake well, strain into shot glasses, and serve.

Serving

Shot Glass <
****

Asthma Attack recipe

Description

A delicious recipe for Asthma Attack, with Everclear® alcohol, Bacardi® 151 rum, DeKuyper® Razzmatazz liqueur and amaretto almond liqueur.

Ingredients

1/2 oz Everclear® alcohol
1/2 oz Bacardi® 151 rum
1/2 oz DeKuyper® Razzmatazz liqueur
1 oz amaretto almond liqueur

Instructions

Shake and serve.

Serving

Highball Glass <
****

Atomic Plum recipe

Description

A delicious recipe for Atomic Plum, with DeKuyper® Peachtree schnapps, Amaretto Di Saronno® liqueur, Bacardi® 151 rum, orange juice, Sprite® soda, cranberry juice and pineapple juice.

Ingredients

1 oz DeKuyper® Peachtree schnapps
1 oz Amaretto Di Saronno® liqueur
1 splash Bacardi® 151 rum
1 splash orange juice
1 splash Sprite® soda
1 splash cranberry juice
1 splash pineapple juice

Instructions

Add all ingredients (except 151 rum) to a cocktail shaker filled with ice cubes and shake vigorously for 15-20 seconds. Pour into a large shot glass, splash with 151 rum and shoot.

Serving

Shot Glass
****

Aussie Beach Blond recipe

Description

A delicious recipe for Aussie Beach Blond, with Bacardi® white rum, Cointreau® orange liqueur, sugar, lime juice, orange juice and passion-fruit.

Ingredients

1 1/2 oz Bacardi® white rum

1 1/4 oz Cointreau® orange liqueur
1 1/2 tsp sugar
3/4 oz lime juice
1 1/4 oz orange juice
1 passion-fruit

Instructions

Combine the rum, Cointreau, lime juice, orange juice, sugar, and the juice from one passion-fruit in a blender with 1/4 cup of crushed ice. Blend and add further crushed ice where needed until slushy consistancy is achieved. Pour into a hurricane glass, garnish with a slice of lemon, lime and orange, and serve.

Serving

Hurricane Glass
****

B.L.T. recipe

Description

A delicious recipe for B.L.T., with Bacardi® Limon rum and iced tea.

Ingredients

1 - 1/2 oz Bacardi® Limon rum
fill with iced tea

Instructions

Fill glass with ice. Add bacardi limon. Fill with iced tea. Add lemon wedge, and serve.

Serving

Collins Glass
****

Bacardi Champagne Punch recipe

Description

A delicious recipe for Bacardi Champagne Punch, with Bacardi® white rum, triple sec, amaretto almond liqueur, grenadine syrup, sugar syrup, pineapple, Champagne and water.

Ingredients

50 cl Bacardi® white rum
10 cl triple sec
10 cl amaretto almond liqueur
5 cl grenadine syrup
5 cl sugar syrup
1 chunked pineapple
150 cl Champagne
1 liter sparkling water

Instructions

Combine ingredients (except champagne and water) in a punch bowl, cover and chill for 2 hours. Add champagne and water, with a little ice. Add 5-10 frozen strawberries. Serve in wine glasses (30 servings).

Serving

White Wine Glass
****

Bacardi Cocktail recipe

Description

A delicious recipe for Bacardi Cocktail, with Bacardi® light rum, lime juice, sugar syrup and grenadine syrup.

Ingredients

1 3/4 oz Bacardi® light rum
1 oz lime juice
1/2 tsp sugar syrup
1 dash grenadine syrup

Instructions

In a shaker half-filled with ice cubes, combine all of the ingredients. Shake well. Strain into a cocktail glass.

Serving

Cocktail Glass
****

Bacardi Confetti Punch recipe

Description

A delicious recipe for Bacardi Confetti Punch, with Bacardi® Carta Blanca white rum, lemonade, grapefruit juice, fruit cocktail and club soda.

Ingredients

750 ml Bacardi® Carta Blanca white rum
6 oz can frozen lemonade
6 oz can frozen grapefruit juice
16 oz can drained fruit cocktail
2 liters chilled club soda

Instructions

In large container, mix all but the soda. Chill for 2 hours, stirring occasionally. When ready to serve, pour over ice in punch bowl, add chilled club soda and stir gently. Makes 8 servings.

Serving

Punch Bowl
****

Bacardi Daug recipe

Description

A delicious recipe for Bacardi Daug, with Hennessy® cognac, Bacardi® silver rum and Coca-Cola®.

Ingredients

1 oz Hennessy® cognac
2 oz Bacardi® silver rum
4 - 6 oz Coca-Cola®

Instructions

Pour the Hennessy cognac into a highball glass half-filled with ice cubes. Add the Bacardi Silver rum, top with the Coca-cola, stir briefly and serve.

Serving

Highball Glass <
****

Bacardi Geezer recipe

Description

A delicious recipe for Bacardi Geezer, with Bacardi Breezer® Lime, vodka, gin, Cointreau® orange liqueur and Archers® peach schnapps.

Ingredients

1 bottle Bacardi Breezer® Lime
1 oz vodka
1 oz gin
1 oz Cointreau® orange liqueur
1 oz Archers® peach schnapps

Instructions

Stir ingredients together in a pint glass, and serve.

Serving

Beer Mug <
****

Bacardi Gold & Cola recipe

Description

A delicious recipe for Bacardi Gold & Cola, with Bacardi® gold rum, Coca-Cola® and lemon.

Ingredients

4 cl Bacardi® gold rum
16 cl Coca-Cola®

1 slice lemon

Instructions

Fill a tall glass completely with ice cubes. Mix the ingredients into the glass and serve with a slice of lemon put on the glass. It is a very simple drink, but never the less it is very delicious - especially in the summertime.

Serving

Collins Glass
****

Bacardi Hawaiian Punch recipe

Description

A delicious recipe for Bacardi Hawaiian Punch, with Bacardi® Limon rum, Bacardi® Razz rum, Bacardi® orange rum, Bacardi® Vanil rum, cranberry juice and pineapple juice.

Ingredients

1/2 oz Bacardi® Limon rum
1/2 oz Bacardi® Razz rum
1/2 oz Bacardi® orange rum
1/2 oz Bacardi® Vanil rum
3 oz cranberry juice
3 oz pineapple juice

Instructions

Pour the Bacardi flavored rums into a cocktail shaker half-filled with ice cubes. Add the cranberry juice and pineapple juice and shake well. Strain into a hurricane glass filled with ice cubes, and serve.

Serving

Hurricane Glass <
****

Bacardi Hurricane recipe

Description

A delicious recipe for Bacardi Hurricane, with Bacardi® white rum, Bacardi® black rum and passion-fruit syrup.

Ingredients

3/4 oz Bacardi® white rum
3/4 oz Bacardi® black rum
3/4 oz passion-fruit syrup

Instructions

Shake and strain into a hurricane glass filled with crushed ice. Garnish with a slice of lime, and serve.

Serving

Hurricane Glass <
****

Bacardi Martini recipe

Description

A delicious recipe for Bacardi Martini, with Bacardi® white rum and dry vermouth.

Ingredients

2 1/2 oz Bacardi® white rum
1/2 oz dry vermouth

Instructions

Stir and strain into a frosted cocktail glass. Serve with a green olive.

Serving

Cocktail Glass
****

Bacardi O Coffee recipe

Description

A delicious recipe for Bacardi O Coffee, with Bacardi® orange rum, coffee, Irish cream and green creme de menthe.

Ingredients

2 oz Bacardi® orange rum
3 oz hot coffee
1 splash Irish cream
1 splash green creme de menthe

Instructions

Add bacardi O and coffee to a cup. Top with irish cream and green creme de menthe.

****

Bacardi O Tini recipe

Description

A delicious recipe for Bacardi O Tini, with Bacardi® orange rum, pineapple juice and raspberry liqueur.

Ingredients

1 1/2 oz Bacardi® orange rum
3/4 oz pineapple juice

raspberry liqueur

Instructions

Shake bacardi O and pineapple juice, and pour into a chilled glass. Float raspberry liqueur on top.

Serving

Cocktail Glass
****

Bacardi Orange recipe

Description

A delicious recipe for Bacardi Orange, with Bacardi® gold rum, Grand Marnier® orange liqueur, orange juice, soda water and lemonade.

Ingredients

1 3/4 oz Bacardi® gold rum
3/4 oz Grand Marnier® orange liqueur
2 1/2 oz orange juice
1 oz soda water
2 oz lemonade

Instructions

Add to an ice-filled collins glass. Serve with a slice of orange and straws.

Serving

Collins Glass
****

Bacardi Orgasm recipe

Description

A delicious recipe for Bacardi Orgasm, with Bacardi® orange rum and V8 Splash® fruit juice.

Ingredients

1 1/2 oz Bacardi® orange rum
6 oz V8 Splash® fruit juice

Instructions

Pour both ingredients into a highball glass 3/4 filled with ice cubes. Stir well, and serve.

Serving

Highball Glass
****

Bacardi Pina Colada recipe

Description

A delicious recipe for Bacardi Pina Colada, with coconut cream, pineapple juice and Bacardi® white rum.

Ingredients

1 oz coconut cream
2 oz pineapple juice
1 1/2 oz Bacardi® white rum

Instructions

Frappe and pour into a cocktail glass.

Serving

Cocktail Glass <
****

Bacardi Pink recipe

Description

A delicious recipe for Bacardi Pink, with Bacardi® Limon rum and Minute Maid® pink lemonade.

Ingredients

4 oz Bacardi® Limon rum
8 oz Minute Maid® pink lemonade

Instructions

Pour Bacardi Limon rum straight into a collins glass half-filled with ice cubes. Add Minute Maid pink lemonade. Stir with a straw, and serve.

Serving

Collins Glass <
****

Bacardi Refresher recipe

Description

A delicious recipe for Bacardi Refresher, with Bacardi® white rum, sweet and sour mix and grenadine syrup.

Ingredients

1 1/2 oz Bacardi® white rum
3 oz sweet and sour mix
1 splash grenadine syrup

Instructions

Shake ingredients together with cracked ice in a cocktail shaker. Strain into an old-fashioned glass over ice cubes. Garnish with a maraschino cherry and orange slice, and serve.

Serving

Cocktail Glass
****

Bacardi Remix recipe

Description

A delicious recipe for Bacardi Remix, with Sprite Remix and Bacardi® orange rum.

Ingredients

12 oz Sprite Remix
1 - 1 1/2 oz Bacardi® orange rum

Instructions

Pour a glass of sprite remix into a large highball glass or any other good useful cup then add Bacardi O. Stir, add a twist or piece of orange for flavor, and serve.

Serving

Highball Glass <

****

Bacardi Rootbeer Float recipe

Description

A delicious recipe for Bacardi Rootbeer Float, with Bacardi® Vanil rum and root beer.

Ingredients

1 part Bacardi® Vanil rum
2 parts root beer

Instructions

Combine and mix together the rum and root beer in a beer mug. Add ice if desired, and serve.

Serving

Beer Mug

****

Bacardi Special recipe

Description

A delicious recipe for Bacardi Special, with Bacardi® white rum, gin, limes, grenadine syrup and sugar.

Ingredients

2 oz Bacardi® white rum
3/4 oz gin
juice of 1 small limes

1 dash grenadine syrup
1 tsp sugar

Instructions

Shake all but rum with ice until cold. Add rum and shake again. Strain into a cocktail glass.

Serving

Cocktail Glass
****

Bacardi Stinger recipe

Description

A delicious recipe for Bacardi Stinger, with amaretto almond liqueur, Bacardi® 151 rum and Coca-Cola®.

Ingredients

1 part amaretto almond liqueur
1 part Bacardi® 151 rum
2 parts Coca-Cola®

Instructions

Add Amaretto and rum, fill with coke, and stir.

Consume slowly, this drink packs a punch.

Serving

Highball Glass <
****

Bacardi Vanilla Coke recipe

Description

A delicious recipe for Bacardi Vanilla Coke, with Bacardi® vanilla rum and Coca-Cola®.

Ingredients

2 oz Bacardi® vanilla rum
12 oz Coca-Cola®

Instructions

Pour the Bacardi vanilla rum into a collins glass 1/3 filled with ice. Fill the rest of the glass with Coca-cola, and serve.

Serving

Collins Glass <
****

Bacardi Volcano recipe

Description

A delicious recipe for Bacardi Volcano, with limes, Coca-Cola®, Bacardi® 151 rum and Everclear® alcohol.

Ingredients

juice of 1/2 limes
1/2 glass Coca-Cola®
1/2 glass Bacardi® 151 rum
1 jigger Everclear® alcohol

Instructions

Put the juice of 1/2 Lime in glass, then pour in cola and bacardi dark. Top up with Everclear. Light. Figure out how to drink it!

Serving

Old-Fashioned Glass
****

Bacardi Yeah Martini Cocktail recipe

Description

A delicious recipe for Bacardi Yeah Martini Cocktail, with Bacardi® orange rum, pineapple juice, cranberry juice, soda and maraschino cherry.

Ingredients

1 1/2 oz Bacardi® orange rum
2 1/2 oz pineapple juice
1 1/2 oz cranberry juice
1 splash soda
1 maraschino cherry

Instructions

Serve in a chilled glass garnished with a lime and maraschino cherry.

****

Bacardi-ade recipe

Description

A delicious recipe for Bacardi-ade, with Bacardi® Limon rum, lemonade and lemon juice.

Ingredients

3 oz Bacardi® Limon rum
2 oz lemonade
1/2 oz lemon juice

Instructions

Stir ingredients together in a highball glass with ice cubes, and serve.

Serving

Highball Glass
****

Backfire On The Freeway recipe

Description

A delicious recipe for Backfire On The Freeway, with Bacardi® 151 rum and Guinness® stout.

Ingredients

2 oz Bacardi® 151 rum
6 oz Guinness® stout

Instructions

Drop a double shot of 151 into a beer mug of guinness and chug immediately.

Serving

Beer Mug
****

Ba-dew-si recipe

Description

A delicious recipe for Ba-dew-si, with Bacardi® 151 rum, Pepsi® cola and Mountain Dew® lime soda.

Ingredients

2 oz Bacardi® 151 rum
5 oz chilled Pepsi® cola
5 oz chilled Mountain Dew® lime soda

Instructions

Stir ingredients together in a highball glass, and serve.

Serving

Highball Glass
****

Bahama Todd recipe

Description

A delicious recipe for Bahama Todd, with light rum, dark rum, spiced rum, Malibu® coconut rum, Bacardi® 151 rum, Blue Curacao liqueur and pineapple juice.

Ingredients

1/2 oz light rum
1/2 oz dark rum
1/2 oz spiced rum
1/2 oz Malibu® coconut rum
1/2 oz Bacardi® 151 rum
1/2 oz Blue Curacao liqueur
5 oz pineapple juice

Instructions

Add light rum, dark rum, spiced rum, and malibu rum to an ice-filled glass. Mix in pineapple juice and blue curacao. Float 151 rum on top, and serve.

Serving

Collins Glass
****

Bali Dream recipe

Description

A delicious recipe for Bali Dream, with Bacardi® white rum, Bacardi® black rum, creme de bananes, Passoa® liqueur, coconut liqueur, grenadine syrup and orange juice.

Ingredients

20 cl Bacardi® white rum
20 cl Bacardi® black rum
20 cl creme de bananes
20 cl Passoa® liqueur
10 cl coconut liqueur
10 cl grenadine syrup
200 cl orange juice

Instructions

Put all ingredients in shaker together with some ice-cubes. Shake well. Serve with piece of banana on top of the glass.

Serving

Cocktail Glass
****

Ball of Fun recipe

Description

A delicious recipe for Ball of Fun, with Bacardi® Limon rum, triple sec, Absolut® Citron vodka, fruit punch and ice cubes.

Ingredients

1 liter Bacardi® Limon rum
1 liter triple sec
1 liter Absolut® Citron vodka
2 liters fruit punch
5 lb ice cubes

Instructions

Pour all ingredients into a punch bowl and stir."Drink the fuck up, get fucked up, and break the ball of fun." (BSU)

Serving

Punch Bowl
****

Barking Spider recipe

Description

A delicious recipe for Barking Spider, with Tarantula Azul Tequila, Blue Curacao liqueur, Bacardi® 151 rum, triple sec, sweet and sour mix and orange juice.

Ingredients

1 1/2 oz Tarantula Azul Tequila
1 1/2 oz Blue Curacao liqueur
3/4 oz Bacardi® 151 rum
1 dash triple sec
1 dash sweet and sour mix
1 splash orange juice

Instructions

Serve over ice in a collins glass, or blend for a frozen version of this drink.

Serving

Collins Glass
****

Bastardized Screwdriver recipe

Description

A delicious recipe for Bastardized Screwdriver, with Bacardi® gold rum, Tropicana® orange juice and ice.

Ingredients

3 parts Bacardi® gold rum
1 part Tropicana® orange juice
ice

Instructions

Ice, then rum, then orange juice. Mix.

****

Battery Skydiver recipe

Description

A delicious recipe for Battery Skydiver, with Bacardi® 151 rum, Bacardi® silver rum, Blue Curacao liqueur and lime juice.

Ingredients

1 oz Bacardi® 151 rum
1 1/2 oz Bacardi® silver rum
1/2 oz Blue Curacao liqueur
1/2 oz lime juice

Instructions

Mix all ingredients together with an ice cube or two, shaking vigorously and pour into a highball glass over 3 - 5 ice cubes. Serve.

Serving

Highball Glass
****

Bazooka Joe #2 recipe

Description

A delicious recipe for Bazooka Joe #2, with Bacardi® Limon rum and Red Bull® energy drink.

Ingredients

2 oz Bacardi® Limon rum
8 oz Red Bull® energy drink

Instructions

Pour the Bacardi limon into a collins glass. Add a small, 8 oz can or thereabouts of Red Bull. Stir well, and serve.

Serving

Collins Glass

****

Beach Bum recipe

Description

A delicious recipe for Beach Bum, with orange juice, Bacardi® Limon rum and Sprite® soda.

Ingredients

1 part orange juice
1 part Bacardi® Limon rum
1 part Sprite® soda

Instructions

Pour into a glass with ice. Stir.

Serving

Highball Glass
****

Beach Cooler recipe

Description

A delicious recipe for Beach Cooler, with Bacardi® 151 rum, Cointreau® orange liqueur, lime juice and papaya nectar.

Ingredients

1 oz Bacardi® 151 rum
1 oz Cointreau® orange liqueur
1 1/2 oz lime juice
2 oz papaya nectar

Instructions

Combine all ingredients in a cocktail shaker half-filled with ice cubes. Shake well, strain into a highball glass filled with ice cubes, and serve.

Serving

Highball Glass
****

Beakers Blue recipe

Description

A delicious recipe for Beakers Blue, with Blue Curacao liqueur, triple sec, Bacardi® Limon rum, Sprite® soda and sweet and sour mix.

Ingredients

1 oz Blue Curacao liqueur

1 oz triple sec

1 oz Bacardi® Limon rum

1 splash Sprite® soda

1 splash sweet and sour mix

Instructions

Add ice cubes, stir, and garnish with cherry.

Serving

Hurricane Glass

****

BearCat Special recipe

Description

A delicious recipe for BearCat Special, with Bacardi® 151 rum and peppermint schnapps.

Ingredients

1/2 shot Bacardi® 151 rum

1/2 shot peppermint schnapps

Instructions

Put both in shot glass, mix, and down.

Serving

Shot Glass

****

Beautiful Disaster recipe

Description

A delicious recipe for Beautiful Disaster, with Bacardi® Limon rum and Sprite® soda.

Ingredients

1 oz Bacardi® Limon rum

2 liters Sprite® soda

Instructions

Empty the mickey into a half-empty bottle of sprite. Put the cap on, and turn upside down slowly a few times - allowing it to mix. Serve in a collins glass with ice.

Serving

Collins Glass

****

Bertiebreezer recipe

Description

A delicious recipe for Bertiebreezer, with apfelkorn liqueur and Bacardi Breezer® Lime.

Ingredients

2 1/2 oz chilled apfelkorn liqueur
3 1/2 oz chilled Bacardi Breezer® Lime

Instructions

Pour the Apfelkorn and Bacardi Breezer over 3 ice cubes in a whiskey sour glass, stir, and serve.

Serving

Whiskey Sour Glass
****

Bird Feeder recipe

Description

A delicious recipe for Bird Feeder, with Yukon Jack® Canadian whisky and Bacardi® 151 rum.

Ingredients

1/2 oz Yukon Jack® Canadian whisky
1/2 oz Bacardi® 151 rum

Instructions

Combine half a shot of each in a shot glass, and serve.

Serving

Shot Glass
****

Black Forest Cake recipe

Description

A delicious recipe for Black Forest Cake, with Kahlua® coffee liqueur, Bacardi® Coco rum, Skyy® vodka and grenadine syrup.

Ingredients

1/2 oz Kahlua® coffee liqueur
1/2 oz Bacardi® Coco rum
1 splash Skyy® vodka
1/4 oz grenadine syrup

Instructions

Layer ingredients in a cocktail glass, and serve.

Serving

Highball Glass
****

Black Rose #2 recipe

Description

A delicious recipe for Black Rose #2, with Bacardi® 151 rum, Green Chartreuse® and Frangelico® hazelnut liqueur.

Ingredients

3/5 oz Bacardi® 151 rum
1/5 oz Green Chartreuse®
1/5 oz Frangelico® hazelnut liqueur

Instructions

Pour the Bacardi 151 into a shot glass. Add the Chartreuse and softly pour the Frangelico liqueur on top for a cloudy efffect before serving.

Serving

Shot Glass
****

Blast Furnace recipe

Description

A delicious recipe for Blast Furnace, with Fire and Ice® vodka, Bacardi® 151 rum and vodka.

Ingredients

1 shot Fire and Ice® vodka
1 shot Bacardi® 151 rum
1 shot vodka

Instructions

Combine ingredients together in a whiskey sour glass, stir, and serve.

Serving

Whiskey Sour Glass
****

Bleacher Creature recipe

Description

A delicious recipe for Bleacher Creature, with butterscotch schnapps and Bacardi® 151 rum.

Ingredients

1 1/2 oz butterscotch schnapps
1 1/2 oz Bacardi® 151 rum

Instructions

Pour butterscotch over rum. Do not stir.

Serving

Shot Glass
****

Bleeding Bacardi recipe

Description

A delicious recipe for Bleeding Bacardi, with Bacardi® Superior rum and raspberry cordial.

Ingredients

2/3 oz Bacardi® Superior rum
1/3 oz raspberry cordial

Instructions

Add the Bacardi first. Then slowly pour in the cordial. Drink when they start to separate.

Serving

Shot Glass
****

Bloated Bag of Monkey Spunk recipe

Description

A delicious recipe for Bloated Bag of Monkey Spunk, with Bacardi® white rum, peach schnapps, Grand Marnier® orange liqueur, pineapple juice and orange juice.

Ingredients

1 oz Bacardi® white rum
1 oz peach schnapps
1/2 oz Grand Marnier® orange liqueur
1 oz pineapple juice
1 oz orange juice

Instructions

Shake and strain into collins glass with ice. Garnish with a cherry.

Serving

Collins Glass
****

Blonde Bombshell recipe

Description

A delicious recipe for Blonde Bombshell, with crushed ice, Bacardi® light rum and lemonade.

Ingredients

2 cups crushed ice
5 shots Bacardi® light rum
1 can frozen lemonade concentrate

Instructions

Add ice, rum, and frozen lemonade concentrate to a blender. Blend at high speed. Pour into a margarita glass.

Serving

Margarita Glass
****

Blonde Moment recipe

Description

A delicious recipe for Blonde Moment, with Bacardi® Limon rum, Blue Curacao liqueur, grenadine syrup, sweet and sour mix and soda water.

Ingredients

1 oz Bacardi® Limon rum
1/2 oz Blue Curacao liqueur
1/3 oz grenadine syrup
1 1/2 oz sweet and sour mix
1 splash soda water

Instructions

Mix over Ice and garnish with a cherry.

Serving

Collins Glass
****

Blonde Ron recipe

Description

A delicious recipe for Blonde Ron, with Bacardi® light rum, 7-Up® soda, ice and pineapple juice.

Ingredients

1 oz Bacardi® light rum
4 oz 7-Up® soda
ice

1 splash pineapple juice

Instructions

Just fill ice, then pour rum, 7up, and slash of pineapple.

Serving

Highball Glass
****

Blood recipe

Description

A delicious recipe for Blood, with Bacardi® white rum and raspberry syrup.

Ingredients

2 oz Bacardi® white rum
1 oz raspberry syrup

Instructions

Pour both ingredients into a Champagne flute filled with crushed or shaven ice. Add more syrup if necessary to obtain a blood red complexion, and serve.

Serving

Champagne Flute
****

Bloody Demon From Hell recipe

Description

A delicious recipe for Bloody Demon From Hell, with Jameson® Irish whiskey, Captain Morgan® Silver spiced rum, Jim Beam® bourbon whiskey, Bacardi® gold rum, tomato juice, Worcestershire sauce and hot pepper sauce. Also list

Ingredients

1 oz Jameson® Irish whiskey
1 oz Captain Morgan® Silver spiced rum
1 oz Jim Beam® bourbon whiskey
1 oz Bacardi® gold rum
2 oz tomato juice
2 oz Worcestershire sauce
1 oz hot pepper sauce

Instructions

Combine all ingredients in a large glass. Garnish with a radish or a celery stick, and serve.

Serving

Highball Glass
****

Blue Bohemian recipe

Description

A delicious recipe for Blue Bohemian, with Becherovka® herbal liqueur, Bacardi® white rum, Blue Curacao liqueur, orange juice and tonic water.

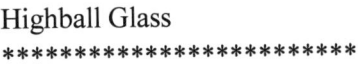

Ingredients

3 parts Becherovka® herbal liqueur
3 parts Bacardi® white rum
1 part Blue Curacao liqueur
5 parts orange juice
tonic water

Instructions

Shake ingredients, garnish with an orange twist and a cherry, and serve.

Serving

Collins Glass
****

Blue Dolphin #2 recipe

Description

A delicious recipe for Blue Dolphin #2, with Bacardi® white rum, Hpnotiq® liqueur and Sprite® soda.

Ingredients

2 oz Bacardi® white rum
2 oz Hpnotiq® liqueur
2 oz Sprite® soda

Instructions

Stir ingredients together in a highball glass filled with ice cubes, and serve.

Serving

Highball Glass
****

Blue Horizon recipe

Description

A delicious recipe for Blue Horizon, with spiced rum, Bacardi® 151 rum, Blue Curacao liqueur, grenadine syrup and orange juice.

Ingredients

3/4 oz spiced rum
3/4 oz Bacardi® 151 rum
3/4 oz Blue Curacao liqueur
1/4 oz grenadine syrup
6 oz orange juice

Instructions

Pour all ingredients into a collins glass almost filled with ice cubes. Garnish with a maraschino cherry, and serve.

Serving

Collins Glass
****

Blue Nuke recipe

Description

A delicious recipe for Blue Nuke, with vodka, Bacardi® 151 rum, gin, Blue Curacao liqueur, blueberry liqueur and sweet and sour mix.

Ingredients

1 oz vodka
1 oz Bacardi® 151 rum
1 oz gin
1 oz Blue Curacao liqueur
1 oz blueberry liqueur
3 - 4 oz sweet and sour mix

Instructions

Pour vodka, Bacardi 151, gin, blue curacao and blueberry liqueur into a collins glass almost filled with ice cubes. Fill with sweet and sour mix, stir well, and serve.

Serving

Collins Glass
****

Blue Smurf Piss recipe

Description

A delicious recipe for Blue Smurf Piss, with Jagermeister® herbal liqueur, ice, Bacardi® 151 rum, Rumple Minze® peppermint liqueur, Goldschlager® cinnamon schnapps and Blue Curacao liqueur.

Ingredients

1/5 shot Jagermeister® herbal liqueur
ice
1/5 shot Bacardi® 151 rum

1/5 shot Rumple Minze® peppermint liqueur

1/5 shot Goldschlager® cinnamon schnapps

1/5 shot Blue Curacao liqueur

Instructions

Pour as listed. Strain through Ice.

Serving

Shot Glass

****

Bo Jo recipe

Description

A delicious recipe for Bo Jo, with Bacardi® white rum, Midori® melon liqueur and fruit punch.

Ingredients

1/3 oz Bacardi® white rum

1/3 oz Midori® melon liqueur

1/3 oz fruit punch

Instructions

Pour the fruit punch into a shot glass. Add the Midori melon liqueur on top, and then follow with the Bacardi white rum, and serve.

Serving

Shot Glass

****

Bomb Pop recipe

Description

A delicious recipe for Bomb Pop, with Bacardi® Razz rum, lemonade and Blue Curacao liqueur.

Ingredients

2 oz Bacardi® Razz rum

2 oz lemonade

2 oz Blue Curacao liqueur

Instructions

Pour the Bacardi Razz rum into a small rocks glass or otherwise. Add blue curacao, and then lemonade, and serve.

Serving

Old-Fashioned Glass

****

Bonsai Pipeline recipe

Description

A delicious recipe for Bonsai Pipeline, with Wild Turkey® 101 bourbon whiskey, melon liqueur and Bacardi® 151 rum.

Ingredients

3/4 oz Wild Turkey® 101 bourbon whiskey
3/4 oz melon liqueur
1/4 oz Bacardi® 151 rum

Instructions

In shoot glass add Wild Turkey and melon liqeur. Float Bacardi 151 on top. Light drink, and squeeze lime in drink. Blow out and shoot.

Serving

Shot Glass
****

Boom Boom Shot recipe

Description

A delicious recipe for Boom Boom Shot, with Bacardi® Limon rum and Sprite® soda.

Ingredients

1/2 oz Bacardi® Limon rum
1/2 oz Sprite® soda

Instructions

Pour Bacardi Limon rum into a shot glass. Add Sprite (or 7-Up). Place a towel on the table and put one hand on top of the shot glass to seal it so that no liquid or gas from the soda escapes. Quickly slam the glass on the towel so that a lot of bubbles are made and consume so that you catch the bubbles going down your throat.

Serving

Shot Glass
****

Booty Juice recipe

Description

A delicious recipe for Booty Juice, with Midori® melon liqueur, Malibu® coconut rum, Bacardi® spiced rum and Bacardi® 151 rum.

Ingredients

1/2 oz Midori® melon liqueur
1/2 oz Malibu® coconut rum

Bacardi® spiced rum
1/4 oz Bacardi® 151 rum

Instructions

Fill mixing glass 1/2 full with ice. Add all ingredients. Strain into a rocks glass.

Serving

Old-Fashioned Glass
****

Brain Fart recipe

Description

A delicious recipe for Brain Fart, with Everclear® alcohol, Smirnoff® Red Label vodka, Mountain Dew® citrus soda, Surge® citrus soda, lemon juice and Bacardi® white rum.

Ingredients

1 fifth Everclear® alcohol
1 fifth Smirnoff® Red Label vodka
2 liters Mountain Dew® citrus soda
2 liters Surge® citrus soda
1 bottle lemon juice
1 pint Bacardi® white rum

Instructions

Pre-chill soda, and mix slowly with other ingredients and ice in a punch bowl.

Serving

Punch Bowl
****

Breath of God recipe

Description

A delicious recipe for Breath of God, with Bacardi® 151 rum, Wild Turkey® 101 bourbon whiskey, Southern Comfort® peach liqueur and grenadine syrup.

Ingredients

1 1/2 oz Bacardi® 151 rum
1 1/2 oz Wild Turkey® 101 bourbon whiskey
1 1/2 oz Southern Comfort® peach liqueur
3/4 oz grenadine syrup

Instructions

Combine all ingredients together in a cocktail glass, stir, and serve.

Breathalizer recipe

Description

A delicious recipe for Breathalizer, with peppermint schnapps and Bacardi® white rum.

Ingredients

1 oz peppermint schnapps
1 oz Bacardi® white rum

Instructions

Mix together and serve.

****

Bronsky recipe

Description

A delicious recipe for Bronsky, with Bacardi® 151 rum, Jose Cuervo® 1800 tequila and sweet and sour mix.

Ingredients

1 1/2 oz Bacardi® 151 rum
1 1/2 oz Jose Cuervo® 1800 tequila
3 oz sweet and sour mix

Instructions

Pour ingredients over ice in a large brandy snifter, and serve.

Serving

Brandy Snifter
****

Brown Eyed Pucker recipe

Description

A delicious recipe for Brown Eyed Pucker, with DeKuyper® Sour Apple Pucker schnapps, Bacardi® 151 rum and Pepsi® cola.

Ingredients

1 - 2 oz DeKuyper® Sour Apple Pucker schnapps

1 - 2 oz Bacardi® 151 rum
12 oz can Pepsi® cola

Instructions

Pour the DeKuyper Sour Apple Pucker into a tall glass. Add the Bacardi 151 rum, then add the Pepsi (alternatively, use Dr. Pepper). Stir and serve.

Serving

Collins Glass
****

Buccaneer recipe

Description

A delicious recipe for Buccaneer, with Corona® Extra lager and Bacardi® Limon rum.

Ingredients

1 can Corona® Extra lager
1 shot Bacardi® Limon rum

Instructions

Pour the corona into an 18oz beer glass pour the bacardi limon into the beer stir very gently.

Serving

Beer Mug
****

Buffalo Chip recipe

Description

A delicious recipe for Buffalo Chip, with Bacardi® 151 rum and Wild Turkey® bourbon whiskey.

Ingredients

1/2 oz Bacardi® 151 rum
1/2 oz Wild Turkey® bourbon whiskey

Instructions

Pour both ingredients into a shot glass, and shoot.

Serving

Shot Glass
****

Buffalo Sweat recipe

Description

A delicious recipe for Buffalo Sweat, with Bacardi® 151 rum, Tabasco® sauce and orange juice.

Ingredients

3/4 oz Bacardi® 151 rum
1/4 oz Tabasco® sauce
1 oz orange juice

Instructions

Pour 151 proof rum and tabasco sauce into a stainless shaker over ice, shake until completely cold and strain into an old-fashioned glass. Pour a 1/4 cup of orange juice over the bar, clean up with the bar rag then squeeze 1 oz. out of bar rag into the drink.
Serve to your nastiest customer.

Serving

Old-Fashioned Glass
****

Burning Demon Piss recipe

Description

A delicious recipe for Burning Demon Piss, with Jose Cuervo® Especial gold tequila, Southern Comfort® peach liqueur, Captain Morgan® Original spiced rum, Kahlua® coffee liqueur, hot pepper sauce, coffee and Bacardi®

Ingredients

1 oz Jose Cuervo® Especial gold tequila
3 oz Southern Comfort® peach liqueur
1 oz Captain Morgan® Original spiced rum
1 oz Kahlua® coffee liqueur
3 oz hot pepper sauce
6 oz burning hot coffee
1 1/2 oz Bacardi® white rum

Instructions

Pour the Jose Cuervo tequila, Southern Comfort peach liqueur, Captain Morgan spiced rum and Kahlua coffee liqueur into a beer mug. Add hot sauce and an extremely hot cup of coffee, then top with Bacardi and serve.

Serving

Beer Mug
****

Bushwacker recipe

Description

A delicious recipe for Bushwacker, with cream of coconut, Kahlua® coffee liqueur, Bacardi® black rum, dark creme de cacao and milk.

Ingredients

4 oz cream of coconut
2 oz Kahlua® coffee liqueur
1 oz Bacardi® black rum
1 oz dark creme de cacao
4 oz milk

Instructions

Combine ingredients with two cups of ice in a blender. Blend until smooth, and serve up in two 12 oz cups.

Serving

Cup
****

CA Area 151 recipe

Description

A delicious recipe for CA Area 151, with amaretto almond liqueur, Bacardi® 151 rum, sweet and sour mix and ice.

Ingredients

1 oz amaretto almond liqueur
1 oz Bacardi® 151 rum
1 oz sweet and sour mix
ice

Instructions

Fill cup with ice. Add equal parts of all ingredients. Stir. Serve immediately.

Serving

Whiskey Sour Glass
****

Camel Piss recipe

Description

A delicious recipe for Camel Piss, with Canadian beer, tequila, Bacardi® dark rum, ouzo anise liqueur and Mountain Dew® citrus soda.

Ingredients

3 oz Canadian beer
2 oz tequila
1 oz Bacardi® dark rum
1 oz ouzo anise liqueur
Mountain Dew® citrus soda

Instructions

Pour the beer, tequila, dark rum and ouzo into a highball glass. Top with mountain dew, to taste, and serve.

Serving

Highball Glass
****

Candy Cocktail recipe

Description

A delicious recipe for Candy Cocktail, with Dr. Pepper® soda, Bacardi® 151 rum and amaretto almond liqueur.

Ingredients

12 oz Dr. Pepper® soda
1 1/4 oz Bacardi® 151 rum
3/4 oz amaretto almond liqueur

Instructions

Fill a tall glass with ice. Pour the 151 proof rum, dr. pepper and amaretto, stir, and serve.

Serving

Collins Glass
****

Captain Jack Sparrow recipe

Description

A delicious recipe for Captain Jack Sparrow, with Bacardi® 151 rum, Captain Morgan® Original spiced rum, Southern Comfort® peach liqueur and pineapple juice.

Ingredients

1 1/2 oz Bacardi® 151 rum
2 oz Captain Morgan® Original spiced rum
2 oz Southern Comfort® peach liqueur
9 oz pineapple juice

Instructions

Empty a 16 ounce bottle and add 6 ice cubes to it. Add the Bacardi 151 rum, Captain Morgan Original spiced rum, Southern Comfort and pineapple juice. Leave enough room at the top for the foam when you shake it up. Shake until ice cubes are pretty much melted and serve. May be served on ice if desired.

Serving

Old-Fashioned Glass
****

Cardicas recipe

Description

A delicious recipe for Cardicas, with Bacardi® white rum, Cointreau® orange liqueur and white port.

Ingredients

2 cl Bacardi® white rum
1 cl Cointreau® orange liqueur
1 cl white port

Instructions

Stir. No garnish.

Serving

Cocktail Glass
****

Caribbean Breeze recipe

Description

A delicious recipe for Caribbean Breeze, with Bacardi® 151 rum, Malibu® coconut rum, pineapple juice and cranberry juice.

Ingredients

1 oz Bacardi® 151 rum
1/2 oz Malibu® coconut rum
fill with 1/2 pineapple juice
fill with 1/2 cranberry juice

Instructions

Pour ingredients into a Collins glass filled with ice. Stir and serve!

Serving

Collins Glass
****

Caribbean Ice Tea recipe

Description

A delicious recipe for Caribbean Ice Tea, with Blue Curacao liqueur, gin, Bacardi® white rum, Jose Cuervo® Especial gold tequila, Absolut® vodka and sweet and sour mix.

Ingredients

1 part Blue Curacao liqueur
1 part gin
1 part Bacardi® white rum
1 part Jose Cuervo® Especial gold tequila
1 part Absolut® vodka

1 part sweet and sour mix

Instructions

Mix all of the ingredients together and serve over ice. Garnish with an orange.

Serving

Hurricane Glass
****

Caribbean Murder recipe

Description

A delicious recipe for Caribbean Murder, with RedRum® rum, Malibu® coconut rum, Bacardi® Limon rum, pineapple juice, cranberry juice and grenadine syrup.

Ingredients

1 oz RedRum® rum
1/2 oz Malibu® coconut rum
1/2 oz Bacardi® Limon rum
3 oz pineapple juice
3 oz cranberry juice
1 splash grenadine syrup

Instructions

Pour the Redrum, Malibu rum and Bacardi Limon rum into a collins glass filled with ice cubes. Add the fruit juice, and top with grenadine. Garnish with a slice of lime, and serve.

Serving

Collins Glass
****

Caribe Cosmopolitan recipe

Description

A delicious recipe for Caribe Cosmopolitan, with Bacardi® Limon rum, cranberry juice, Cointreau® orange liqueur and lime juice.

Ingredients

1 1/2 oz Bacardi® Limon rum
1 oz cranberry juice
1 oz Cointreau® orange liqueur
1/2 oz fresh lime juice

Instructions

Shake all ingredients with ice and strain into a chilled martini glass. Garnish with flamed orange peel, and serve.

Serving

Cocktail Glass
****

Carolina Dream recipe

Description

A delicious recipe for Carolina Dream, with Bacardi® white rum, cream of coconut, pineapple juice, peach, lime juice, sugar and Grand Marnier® orange liqueur.

Ingredients

6 oz Bacardi® white rum
4 oz cream of coconut
4 oz pineapple juice
1 peach
1 tbsp lime juice
1/2 tbsp sugar
1 oz Grand Marnier® orange liqueur

Instructions

Blend with two cups of ice, until all chunks of peach and ice are gone.

This drink was inspired by the intense heat of the fourth of july in the south east.

Serving

Margarita Glass
****

Cave In recipe

Description

A delicious recipe for Cave In, with amaretto almond liqueur, Bacardi® 151 rum, Southern Comfort® peach liqueur, orange juice and cranberry juice.

Ingredients

1 oz amaretto almond liqueur
1 oz Bacardi® 151 rum
1 oz Southern Comfort® peach liqueur
1 splash orange juice
cranberry juice

Instructions

Pour the amaretto, Bacardi 151 and Southern Comfort into an old-fashioned glass 3/4 filled with ice cubes. Stir well. Add cranberry juice to taste, and stir again briefly. Add a splash of orange juice, and serve.

Serving

Old-Fashioned Glass
****

Cemetary Cider recipe

Description

A delicious recipe for Cemetary Cider, with Captain Morgan® Silver spiced rum, Jim Beam® bourbon whiskey, Bacardi® orange rum and apple cider.

Ingredients

2 oz Captain Morgan® Silver spiced rum
2 oz Jim Beam® bourbon whiskey
2 oz Bacardi® orange rum
12 oz apple cider

Instructions

Combine the rums and whiskey over ice in a cocktail shaker. Shake well. Add the apple cider and stir lightly. Pour into a pint glass, and serve.

Serving

Beer Mug
****

Cha Cha Unocha recipe

Description

A delicious recipe for Cha Cha Unocha, with UV® blue raspberry vodka, Bacardi® Superior rum, Sprite® soda and Malibu® coconut rum.

Ingredients

1/3 oz UV® blue raspberry vodka
1/3 oz Bacardi® Superior rum
1/6 oz Sprite® soda
1/6 oz Malibu® coconut rum

Instructions

Build ingredients in order in a shot glass, and shoot.

Serving

Shot Glass
****

Chaise Lounge recipe

Description

A delicious recipe for Chaise Lounge, with Bacardi® Limon rum, Malibu® coconut rum, creme de bananes, cranberry juice, orange juice and pineapple juice.

Ingredients

1 1/2 oz Bacardi® Limon rum
1 1/2 oz Malibu® coconut rum
1 1/2 oz creme de bananes
2 splashes cranberry juice
2 splashes orange juice
2 dashes pineapple juice

Instructions

Pour the Bacardi Limon, Malibu rum, creme de bananes and juices into a cocktail shaker half-filled with ice cubes. Shake well. Strain into a highball glass half-filled with ice cubes, and serve.

Serving

Highball Glass
****

Cherry Bomb #7 recipe

Description

A delicious recipe for Cherry Bomb #7, with Bacardi® 151 rum and grenadine syrup.

Ingredients

1 1/2 oz Bacardi® 151 rum
1 1/2 oz grenadine syrup

Instructions

Pour the grenadine into a shot glass, then carefully pour the Bacardi 151 on top; the two should not mix. Light it on fire, blow out the flames and shoot.

Serving

Shot Glass
****

Cherry Popper #4 recipe

Description

A delicious recipe for Cherry Popper #4, with Bacardi® vanilla rum and black cherry soda.

Ingredients

2 oz Bacardi® vanilla rum
8 oz black cherry soda

Instructions

Stir ingredients together in a collins glass almost filled   with ice cubes, and serve.

Serving

Collins Glass
****

Chicago View recipe

Description

A delicious recipe for Chicago View, with Bacardi® orange rum, raspberry liqueur and passion-fruit juice.

Ingredients

2 oz Bacardi® orange rum
1/2 oz raspberry liqueur
2 oz passion-fruit juice

Instructions

Shake with ice and serve over ice.

Serving

Highball Glass
****

China Village Mai Tai recipe

Description

A delicious recipe for China Village Mai Tai, with Bacardi® dark rum, Bacardi® light rum, triple sec, Tropicana® orange juice, pineapple juice, grenadine syrup and ice cubes.

Ingredients

1 oz Bacardi® dark rum
1 oz Bacardi® light rum
1 1/2 oz triple sec
1/2 oz Tropicana® orange juice
1 oz canned pineapple juice
1/4 oz grenadine syrup
ice cubes

Instructions

In a metal shaker add a fair amount of ice cubes. Add dark rum and light rum, then grenadine, orange juice, and pineapple juice. Finally add triple sec and shake vigorously.

Pour in a thick tall ribbed glass. Top with a cherry or a dash of triple sec.

Serving

Collins Glass
****

Chocolate Coke recipe

Description

A delicious recipe for Chocolate Coke, with Bacardi® white rum, Kahlua® coffee liqueur and Coca-Cola®.

Ingredients

2 oz Bacardi® white rum
2 oz Kahlua® coffee liqueur
6 oz Coca-Cola®

Instructions

Pour the Bacardi white rum and Kahlua coffee liqueur into a collins glass filled with ice cubes. Fill with Coca-cola, and serve.

Serving

Collins Glass
****

Chocolate Pirate recipe

Description

A delicious recipe for Chocolate Pirate, with Bacardi® 151 rum, Kahlua® coffee liqueur, milk and chocolate ice cream.

Ingredients

1 1/2 oz Bacardi® 151 rum
1 oz Kahlua® coffee liqueur
1 oz milk
2 scoops chocolate ice cream

Instructions

Blend ingredients in a blender until smooth. Serve in a chilled wine goblet.

Serving

Wine Goblet
****

ChoozyMothers Milk recipe

Description

A delicious recipe for ChoozyMothers Milk, with milk, Bacardi® 151 rum, Bacardi® white rum, vanilla ice cream, cinnamon and Kahlua® coffee liqueur.

Ingredients

5 gal milk
1 gal Bacardi® 151 rum

1 gal Bacardi® white rum
5 gal vanilla ice cream
10 oz powdered cinnamon
1 fifth Kahlua® coffee liqueur

Instructions

In a large kettle (lobster pot), mix the Bacardi 151 Dark Rum, Bacardi White Rum, Kahlua, Milk and Vanilla Ice Cream (keep the ice cream in its form from the carton). Stir and mix in the cinnamon powder.

Serving

Mason Jar
****

Chris Anders Shot recipe

Description

A delicious recipe for Chris Anders Shot, with Bacardi® O rum, cranberry juice and lemon-lime soda.

Ingredients

1 1/2 oz Bacardi® O rum
1 splash cranberry juice
1 splash lemon-lime soda

Instructions

Shake all ingredients together in a cocktail shaker with a few ice cubes. Strain into a 2-oz shot glass and serve.

Serving

Shot Glass
****

Cina Polada recipe

Description

A delicious recipe for Cina Polada, with Bacardi® 151 rum, 99 Bananas® banana schnapps and pina colada mix.

Ingredients

1 oz Bacardi® 151 rum
1 oz 99 Bananas® banana schnapps
3 oz pina colada mix

Instructions

Blend with 2 cups of ice until smooth. Pour into hurricane glass and garnish with pineapple wedge and banana slice.

Serving

Hurricane Glass

****

Citrus Coke recipe

Description

A delicious recipe for Citrus Coke, with Bacardi® Limon rum and Coca-Cola®.

Ingredients

1 part Bacardi® Limon rum
2 parts Coca-Cola®

Instructions

Pour half of a can of coke into a tall glass. Add bacardi limon, and top off with the remaining coke. Stir and serve.

Serving

Collins Glass
****

Citrus Surprise recipe

Description

A delicious recipe for Citrus Surprise, with Bacardi® Limon rum and Squirt® citrus soda.

Ingredients

1/4 glass Bacardi® Limon rum
3/4 glass Squirt® citrus soda

Instructions

Mix together in a tall glass, and serve.

Serving

Collins Glass
****

Clear Cell recipe

Description

A delicious recipe for Clear Cell, with lemon vodka, Bacardi® Limon rum, tequila, dry gin and lemon-lime soda.

Ingredients

1 oz lemon vodka
1 oz Bacardi® Limon rum
1 oz tequila
1 oz dry gin
2 oz lemon-lime soda

Instructions

Pour the lemon vodka, lemon rum, tequila and gin into a cocktail shaker half-filled with ice cubes. Shake well, and strain into a highball glass filled with ice cubes. Top with lemon-lime soda, garnish with a lime wedge, and serve.

Serving

Highball Glass
****

Closed Casket recipe

Description

A delicious recipe for Closed Casket, with Jagermeister® herbal liqueur, Bacardi® 151 rum, Firewater® cinnamon schnapps and Rumple Minze® peppermint liqueur.

Ingredients

1 oz Jagermeister® herbal liqueur
1 oz Bacardi® 151 rum
1/4 oz Firewater® cinnamon schnapps
1/4 oz Rumple Minze® peppermint liqueur

Instructions

Pour 151 last and light.

Serving

Shot Glass
****

Coast Colada recipe

Description

A delicious recipe for Coast Colada, with Bacardi® white rum, Midori® melon liqueur, pina colada mix, banana and crushed ice.

Ingredients

1 oz Bacardi® white rum
3/4 oz Midori® melon liqueur
3 oz pina colada mix
1/3 fresh banana
1 1/2 scoops crushed ice

Instructions

Blend all ingredients together in a blender. Pour into a hurricane glass garnished with a slice of starfruit, and serve.

Serving

Hurricane Glass
****

Coco Martini recipe

Description

A delicious recipe for Coco Martini, with Bacardi® Coco rum, Kahlua® coffee liqueur and brown creme de cacao.

Ingredients

1 1/2 oz Bacardi® Coco rum
3/4 oz Kahlua® coffee liqueur
1/2 oz brown creme de cacao

Instructions

Pour Bacardi Coco, Kahlua and brown creme de cacao into a mixing glass. Shake, and strain into a cocktail/martini glass. Spiral chocolate syrup from the center to the outer rim. Garnish with a chocolate spiral, and serve.

Serving

Cocktail Glass
****

Cold Hearted Threesome recipe

Description

A delicious recipe for Cold Hearted Threesome, with Bacardi® Coco rum, peach schnapps, Bacardi® white rum, orange juice, cranberry juice, pineapple juice, grenadine syrup and crushed ice.

Ingredients

1 oz Bacardi® Coco rum
1 oz peach schnapps
1/2 oz Bacardi® white rum
1 oz orange juice
1 oz cranberry juice
1 oz pineapple juice
1 oz grenadine syrup
1 cup crushed ice

Instructions

Add all ingredients to a blender. Blend until smooth. Pour into a hurricane glass, and serve.

Serving

Hurricane Glass
****

College Hulk Punch recipe

Description

A delicious recipe for College Hulk Punch, with Bacardi® 151 rum, Blue Curacao liqueur, sweet and sour mix and Tropicana® orange juice.

Ingredients

1 L Bacardi® 151 rum
1 L Blue Curacao liqueur
1 L sweet and sour mix
Tropicana® orange juice

Instructions

Add half bowl of ice to a punch bowl. Add the Bacardi 151 and Blue Curacao, and mix with the ice. Add the sweet and sour mix.

Add orange juice until smooth to the taste and a really green cool color like the incredible hulk.

Serving

Punch Bowl
****

Cool Paradise recipe

Description

A delicious recipe for Cool Paradise, with Bacardi® orange rum, peppermint schnapps, spiced rum and Sprite® soda.

Ingredients

1 1/2 oz Bacardi® orange rum
1 1/2 oz peppermint schnapps
3/4 oz spiced rum
4 oz Sprite® soda

Instructions

Combine all of the ingredients in an old-fashioned glass filled with ice cubes, and serve.

Serving

Old-Fashioned Glass
****

Cordial Cooler recipe

Description

A delicious recipe for Cordial Cooler, with Bacardi® white rum, rock melon, pineapple, sugar and orange squash.

Ingredients

1 1/2 oz Bacardi® white rum
3 rock melon chunk
3 pineapple chunk
1 tbsp sugar
orange squash

Instructions

Muddle rockmelon and pineapple chunks with sugar in the bottom of a highball glass. Add Bacardi white rum and a few ice cubes. Top with orange squash (premixed with water as per normal cordial ratio).

Serving

Highball Glass
****

Crack Pipe recipe

Description

A delicious recipe for Crack Pipe, with Bacardi® 151 rum, Rumple Minze® peppermint liqueur and Wild Turkey® bourbon whiskey.

Ingredients

1 oz Bacardi® 151 rum
1 oz Rumple Minze® peppermint liqueur
1 oz Wild Turkey® bourbon whiskey

Instructions

Shake with ice, strain into glass.

Serving

Highball Glass
****

Crazy Dave recipe

Description

A delicious recipe for Crazy Dave, with Skyy® vodka, Bacardi® gold rum, sweet and sour mix, Bacardi® 151 rum and cosmopolitan mix.

Ingredients

1/2 oz Skyy® vodka
1/4 oz Bacardi® gold rum
1/4 oz sweet and sour mix
1/4 oz Bacardi® 151 rum
1/2 oz cosmopolitan mix

Instructions

Pour all ingredients into a cocktail shaker half-filled with ice cubes. Shake well, strain into a double-shot glass, and serve.

Serving

Shot Glass
****

Crimson Tide recipe

Description

A delicious recipe for Crimson Tide, with Absolut® vodka, Malibu® coconut rum, Chambord® raspberry liqueur, Maui® Blue Hawaiian schnapps, Southern Comfort® peach liqueur, Bacardi® 151 rum, cranberry juice an

Ingredients

1/4 oz Absolut® vodka
1/4 oz Malibu® coconut rum
1/4 oz Chambord® raspberry liqueur
1/4 oz Maui® Blue Hawaiian schnapps
1/4 oz Southern Comfort® peach liqueur
1/4 oz Bacardi® 151 rum
1/4 oz cranberry juice
1/4 oz Sprite® soda

Instructions

Combine all ingrediants, chill over ice, strain.

****

Crocodile recipe

Description

A delicious recipe for Crocodile, with Midori® melon liqueur, Bacardi® Limon rum and Sprite® soda.

Ingredients

2 oz Midori® melon liqueur
1 oz Bacardi® Limon rum
Sprite® soda

Instructions

Pour midori and bacardi over a few ice cubes in a highball glass. Fill the rest of the way with the soda, and give a brisk stir.

Serving

Highball Glass
****

Cruz Azul recipe

Description

A delicious recipe for Cruz Azul, with 151 proof rum, Bacardi® Limon rum, Absolut® Citron vodka, Rumple Minze® peppermint liqueur and Blue Curacao liqueur.

Ingredients

1 oz 151 proof rum
1 oz Bacardi® Limon rum
1 oz Absolut® Citron vodka
1 oz Rumple Minze® peppermint liqueur
1 oz Blue Curacao liqueur

Instructions

Stir and serve.

Serving

Shot Glass
****

Cuban Assassin recipe

Description

A delicious recipe for Cuban Assassin, with Bacardi® 151 rum, Green Chartreuse® and Tabasco® sauce.

Ingredients

1/2 oz Bacardi® 151 rum
1/2 oz Green Chartreuse®
5 dashes Tabasco® sauce

Instructions

Pour Bacardi 151 rum into a shot glass. Add chartreuse, then 5 or 6 dashes of tabasco sauce, and serve.

Serving

Shot Glass
****

Cuban Crime of Passion recipe

Description

A delicious recipe for Cuban Crime of Passion, with Captain Morgan® Original spiced rum, Bacardi® light rum, Captain Morgan® Parrot Bay coconut rum, triple sec   and pineapple juice.

Ingredients

1 part Captain Morgan® Original spiced rum
1 part Bacardi® light rum
1 part Captain Morgan® Parrot Bay coconut rum
1 part triple sec
1 part pineapple juice

Instructions

Pour all the ingredients into a mixer glass, shake violently, and then pour the mixture into a 12 oz. glass with ice.

Serving

Beer Pilsner
****

Cuban Lemur recipe

Description

A delicious recipe for Cuban Lemur, with Bacardi® 151 rum, Coca-Cola® and limes.

Ingredients

4 oz Bacardi® 151 rum
4 oz Coca-Cola®
3 slices limes

Instructions

Pour Bacardi 151 rum over ice in a highball glass. Add an equal amount of coca-cola. Squeeze in 2 lime slices, and serve.

Serving

Highball Glass
****

Cubano Coffee recipe

Description

A delicious recipe for Cubano Coffee, with Bacardi® white rum, Bols® white creme de cacao, coffee, sugar and double cream.

Ingredients

30 cl Bacardi® white rum
10 cl Bols® white creme de cacao
30 cl hot coffee
3 tsp sugar
20 cl double cream

Instructions

Warm up rum, creme cacao, sugar and coffee. Float the double fresh cream floating on top. Optionally sprinkle some grated chocolate on top of the cream.

Serving

Irish Coffee Cup

****

Dark Side recipe

Description

A delicious recipe for Dark Side, with coconut liqueur, Bacardi® white rum and chocolate syrup.

Ingredients

1/2 oz coconut liqueur
1/2 oz Bacardi® white rum
chocolate syrup

Instructions

Combine the coconut liqueur and Bacardi white rum in a shot glass, stirring to mix. Add just enough syrup to dissolve in it. The syrup should make the drink creamy but liquid enough to go down smoothly.

Serving

Shot Glass

****

Death From Above recipe

Description

A delicious recipe for Death From Above, with Bacardi® 151 rum, Tanqueray® gin and Coca-Cola®.

Ingredients

1 oz Bacardi® 151 rum
1 oz Tanqueray® gin
3 oz Coca-Cola®

Instructions

In a freezingly chilled glass pour in Bacardi 151 and gin. Now light the drink on fire (be extra careful!) After a few seconds of burning the drink, pour in the coke, and serve.

Serving

Old-Fashioned Glass

****

De-Lay recipe

Description

A delicious recipe for De-Lay, with Goldschlager® cinnamon schnapps, Rumple Minze® peppermint liqueur, Bacardi® 151 rum, tequila and grenadine syrup.

Ingredients

1/4 oz Goldschlager® cinnamon schnapps
1/4 oz Rumple Minze® peppermint liqueur
1/4 oz Bacardi® 151 rum
1/4 oz tequila
1 splash grenadine syrup

Instructions

Combine equal amounts of each liquor in a shot glass and stir. Add a splash of grenadine, and serve.

Serving

Shot Glass
****

Detroit Fermi recipe

Description

A delicious recipe for Detroit Fermi, with Bacardi® 151 rum, vodka, Midori® melon liqueur, sweet and sour mix and limes.

Ingredients

2 oz Bacardi® 151 rum
1 oz vodka
1 oz Midori® melon liqueur
1 oz sweet and sour mix
1 squeeze limes

Instructions

Combine all ingredients in an old-fashioned or lowball glass; ignite, extinguish and serve.

Serving

Old-Fashioned Glass
****

DewRunRum recipe

Description

A delicious recipe for DewRunRum, with Bacardi® 151 rum and Mountain Dew® citrus soda.

Ingredients

1 part Bacardi® 151 rum
16 parts Mountain Dew® citrus soda

Instructions

Place two ice cubes into a 16 oz. cup. Add one shot of bacardi 151 proof rum, and pour the mountain dew over the top.

Serving

Cup
****

Dick Hard recipe

Description

A delicious recipe for Dick Hard, with Absolut® vodka, Tanqueray® gin, Bacardi® white rum and Sprite® soda.

Ingredients

1 oz Absolut® vodka
1 oz Tanqueray® gin
1 oz Bacardi® white rum
fill with Sprite® soda

Instructions

Mix all three liquors then fill with sprite. Garnish with lime, and serve.

Serving

Highball Glass
****

Dick in the Dirt recipe

Description

A delicious recipe for Dick in the Dirt, with peach schnapps, Bacardi® 151 rum, Southern Comfort® peach liqueur, Yukon Jack® Canadian whisky, pineapple juice, cranberry juice and Grand Marnier® orange liqueur. Also lists si

Ingredients

1 shot peach schnapps
1/2 shot Bacardi® 151 rum
1/2 shot Southern Comfort® peach liqueur
1/2 shot Yukon Jack® Canadian whisky
1 splash pineapple juice
1 splash cranberry juice
1 splash Grand Marnier® orange liqueur

Instructions

Mix all ingredients in a tall glass on the rocks.

Serving

Collins Glass
****

Dirtiest Ernie recipe

Description

A delicious recipe for Dirtiest Ernie, with Bacardi® 151 rum, Everclear® alcohol and Rumple Minze® peppermint liqueur.

Ingredients

2/3 oz Bacardi® 151 rum
2/3 oz Everclear® alcohol
2/3 oz Rumple Minze® peppermint liqueur

Instructions

Mix the three ingredients in a shot glass and slam.

Serving

Shot Glass
****

Doctor Pepper recipe

Description

A delicious recipe for Doctor Pepper, with draft beer, Bacardi® 151 rum and amaretto almond liqueur.

Ingredients

draft beer
1/4 oz Bacardi® 151 rum
3/4 oz amaretto almond liqueur

Instructions

Place 1/2 of Draft in a mug.
Place 3/4 oz. Amaretto into a shot glass.
Float/Layer 1/4 oz. Bacardi 151 on top of the Amaretto.

Light the Bacardi as to set it on fire.

Quickly drop the shot glass with Amaretto and Bacardi into the Draft Beer and shoot.

Serving

Shot Glass
****

Dominican Goddess recipe

Description

A delicious recipe for Dominican Goddess, with Bacardi® white rum, grapefruit juice and lemon-lime soda.

Ingredients

1 1/2 oz Bacardi® white rum
1/2 oz grapefruit juice
lemon-lime soda

Instructions

Mix ruby red grapefruit juice and lemon-lime vintage seltzer water. Add the rum (as much as desired) and shake.

Serving

Whiskey Sour Glass
****

Donkey Punch recipe

Description

A delicious recipe for Donkey Punch, with orange juice, ginger ale, pineapple juice, Bacardi® light rum and grenadine syrup.

Ingredients

3 parts orange juice
2 parts ginger ale
1 part pineapple juice
1 part Bacardi® light rum
1/4 part grenadine syrup

Instructions

Mix all ingredients in a punchbowl and float orange slices on top.

Serving

Punch Bowl
****

Douglas Slammer recipe

Description

A delicious recipe for Douglas Slammer, with Blue Curacao liqueur, triple sec, vodka, Bacardi® Limon rum and cola.

Ingredients

1 oz Blue Curacao liqueur
1 oz triple sec
1 oz vodka
1 oz Bacardi® Limon rum

4 oz cola

Instructions

Pour all ingredients into a collins glass 2/3 filled with ice cubes. Stir well, and serve.

Serving

Collins Glass
****

Downshift recipe

Description

A delicious recipe for Downshift, with Minute Maid® fruit punch, Sprite® soda, tequila and Bacardi® 151 rum.

Ingredients

2 parts Minute Maid® fruit punch
1 part Sprite® soda
2 shots tequila
Bacardi® 151 rum

Instructions

Start with the sprite. Next comes the tequila. After that, add the Minute Maid fruit punch, then float the 151 proof rum. Rocks optional.

Serving

Hurricane Glass
****

Dr. Bacardi recipe

Description

A delicious recipe for Dr. Bacardi, with Bacardi® white rum and Dr. Pepper® soda.

Ingredients

2 oz Bacardi® white rum
8 oz Dr. Pepper® soda

Instructions

Pour both ingredients into a highball glass with a couple of ice cubes. Stir well, and serve.

Serving

Highball Glass
****

Dr. Pepper #5 recipe

Description

A delicious recipe for Dr. Pepper #5, with amaretto almond liqueur, Bacardi® 151 rum and beer.

Ingredients

1/2 shot amaretto almond liqueur
1/2 shot Bacardi® 151 rum
1/2 glass beer

Instructions

Mix the Amaretto & Bacardi in one shot glass. Fill the beer mug 1/2 way with beer. Light the Bacardi & Amaretto with a match or lighter. Drop the flaming shot glass into the beer. It immediately begins to foam up. At this point gulp it down (be careful not to swallow the shot glass!).

Serving

Beer Mug
****

Dr. Pepper Flame recipe

Description

A delicious recipe for Dr. Pepper Flame, with amaretto almond liqueur, Bacardi® 151 rum and Dr. Pepper® soda.

Ingredients

1 1/2 oz amaretto almond liqueur
1/4 oz Bacardi® 151 rum
8 oz Dr. Pepper® soda

Instructions

Pour the Amaretto almond liqueur into a shot glass leaving at least a quarter-inch of space at the top. Slowly pour the Bacardi 151 rum on top. Have a full cup or glass of Dr. Pepper ready. Ignite the 151 rum in the shot glass, and drop the flaming shot glass into the Dr. Pepper. Drink immediately.

Serving

Shot Glass
****

Dr. Rum recipe

Description

A delicious recipe for Dr. Rum, with Bacardi® 151 rum, Bacardi® vanilla rum and Dr. Pepper® soda.

Ingredients

1/4 oz Bacardi® 151 rum
5 drops Bacardi® vanilla rum
3/4 oz Dr. Pepper® soda

Instructions

Build ingredients in above order in a shot glass, and slam.

Serving

Shot Glass
****

Dreaming in Antalya recipe

Description

A delicious recipe for Dreaming in Antalya, with Bacardi® dark rum, Bacardi® light rum, Cointreau® orange liqueur, lemons, grenadine syrup and ice cubes.

Ingredients

2 cl Bacardi® dark rum
2 cl Bacardi® light rum
2 cl Cointreau® orange liqueur
juice of 1/2 lemons
1 tbsp grenadine syrup
ice cubes

Instructions

Mix in a mixing glass with ice cubes and pour into chilled cocktail glass.

Serving

Cocktail Glass
****

D-Roy recipe

Description

A delicious recipe for D-Roy, with sugar, limes, Bacardi® Limon rum, lemonade and ice cubes.

Ingredients

2 tsp sugar
4 squeezed limes wedges
4 jiggers Bacardi® Limon rum
fill with lemonade
ice cubes

Instructions

Put sugar in glass. Squeeze limes into glass. Stir slightly. Add rum. Add lemonade. Stir and serve.

Serving

Highball Glass
****

Drunken Bunny recipe

Description

A delicious recipe for Drunken Bunny, with Bacardi® orange rum, Blue Curacao liqueur, Midori® melon liqueur and whipped cream.

Ingredients

1 oz Bacardi® orange rum
1 oz Blue Curacao liqueur
1 oz Midori® melon liqueur
1/2 oz whipped cream

Instructions

Blend first three ingredients together in a cocktail glass. The color should turn bright turquoise. Top with whipped cream, and serve.

Serving

Cocktail Glass
****

Drunken Rumsfeld recipe

Description

A delicious recipe for Drunken Rumsfeld, with Bacardi® Razz rum and Rockstar® energy drink.

Ingredients

2 oz Bacardi® Razz rum
6 oz Rockstar® energy drink

Instructions

Pour the Bacardi Razz rum into a highball glass almost filled with ice cubes. Add the Rockstar energy drink, stir and serve.

Serving

Highball Glass
****

El Negro recipe

Description

A delicious recipe for El Negro, with Bacardi® 151 rum, Southern Comfort® peach liqueur and Captain Morgan® spiced rum.

Ingredients

1/3 oz Bacardi® 151 rum
1/3 oz 100 proof Southern Comfort® peach liqueur

1/3 oz Captain Morgan® spiced rum

Instructions

Pour the Bacardi 151 rum into a shot glass. Add the Southern Comfort and Captain Morgan spiced rum; the mixture should turn dark and obtain a fire smell. Serve; beware the delayed hard-hitting bite.

Serving

Shot Glass
****

El Swavo recipe

Description

A delicious recipe for El Swavo, with Bacardi® gold rum, iced tea and sugar.

Ingredients

3 oz Bacardi® gold rum
2 oz iced tea
2 tbsp sugar

Instructions

Stir ingredients together in a highball glass, and serve.

Serving

Highball Glass
****

Electric Watermelon recipe

Description

A delicious recipe for Electric Watermelon, with Tanqueray® Sterling vodka, Bacardi® light rum, Midori® melon liqueur, triple sec, sweet and sour mix, grenadine syrup and 7-Up® soda.

Ingredients

1 part Tanqueray® Sterling vodka
1 part Bacardi® light rum
1 part Midori® melon liqueur
2 splashes triple sec
fill with sweet and sour mix
1 splash grenadine syrup
1 splash 7-Up® soda

Instructions

Add equal parts vodka, rum, and melon liqueur in a tall cocktail glass with ice. Add a couple of splashes of triple sec (orange liquor). Fill to the top with sweet and sour mix. Add a splash of 7-up and grenadine.

Serving

Cocktail Glass
****

Extraterrestrial recipe

Description

A delicious recipe for Extraterrestrial, with Irish cream, Midori® melon liqueur, Stolichnaya® vodka and Bacardi® 151 rum.

Ingredients

1 jigger Irish cream
1 jigger Midori® melon liqueur
1 jigger Stolichnaya® vodka
Bacardi® 151 rum

Instructions

Pour the jigger of Midori first. Layer the Irish Cream on top, then layer the Stoli Vodka. This will give you a very attractive three layer drink.

Optional - add a teaspoon or so of Bacardi 151 on the top of the drink. Then, light the 151 and let burn for 5-10 seconds. Put out with a napkin.

Shoot the drink and enjoy!

****

Fainting Goat recipe

Description

A delicious recipe for Fainting Goat, with Bacardi® Limon rum, Bacardi® Coco rum, Bacardi® vanilla rum, Bacardi® O rum, Bacardi® Razz rum and cranberry juice.

Ingredients

1/2 oz Bacardi® Limon rum
1/2 oz Bacardi® Coco rum
1/2 oz Bacardi® vanilla rum
1/2 oz Bacardi® O rum
1/2 oz Bacardi® Razz rum
1 splash cranberry juice

Instructions

Combine all of the rums into a tumbler with ice. Add enough cranberry to turn the drink a light red color. Shake well and strain into a rocks glass. Shoot.

Serving

Shot Glass
****

Falix recipe

Description

A delicious recipe for Falix, with Bacardi® dark rum, strawberry margarita mix and lemon juice.

Ingredients

2/5 shot Bacardi® dark rum
2/5 shot strawberry margarita mix
1/5 shot lemon juice

Instructions

Pour the bacardi into a shot glass. Add the margarita mix. Top it with the lemon juice and shoot it.

Serving

Shot Glass
****

Fat Frog recipe

Description

A delicious recipe for Fat Frog, with Smirnoff® Ice, Bacardi Breezer® Orange and WKD® Original Vodka Blue.

Ingredients

1 bottle Smirnoff® Ice
1 bottle Bacardi Breezer® Orange
1 bottle WKD® Original Vodka Blue

Instructions

Get 2 pint glasses, pour one half of Smirnoff Ice into one pint glass and the rest in the other glass, then do the same with the orange breezer, then followed by the Blue WKD. Mix, and the drink should turn green. Add ice as desired, and serve.

Serving

Beer Mug
****

Fat Titties recipe

Description

A delicious recipe for Fat Titties, with Bacardi® Limon rum, Sprite® soda and Ocean Spray Kiwi-Strawberry

Juice.

Ingredients

3 oz Bacardi® Limon rum
3 oz Sprite® soda
3 oz Ocean Spray Kiwi-Strawberry Juice

Instructions

Stir ingredients over a few ice cubes in a highball glass, and serve.

Serving

Highball Glass
****

Fatass recipe

Description

A delicious recipe for Fatass, with Stoli® Razberi vodka and Bacardi® Limon rum.

Ingredients

1/2 oz Stoli® Razberi vodka
1/2 oz Bacardi® Limon rum

Instructions

Pour Stoli raspberry vodka and Bacardi Limon into a shot glass in equal parts, and serve.

Serving

Shot Glass
****

FDU Spanish recipe

Description

A delicious recipe for FDU Spanish, with Bacardi® Limon rum and Hpnotiq® liqueur.

Ingredients

1/2 oz Bacardi® Limon rum
1/2 oz Hpnotiq® liqueur

Instructions

Pour Hpnotiq into a shot glass. Add an equal amount of Bacardi Limon rum, stir, and serve.

Serving

Shot Glass
****

Fiery Balls Of Death recipe

Description

A delicious recipe for Fiery Balls Of Death, with Bacardi® 151 rum, Everclear® alcohol and triple sec.

Ingredients

1/3 shot Bacardi® 151 rum
1/3 shot Everclear® alcohol
1/3 shot triple sec

Instructions

Pour ingredients into a shot glass. Ignite, pray for your life and down it.

Serving

Shot Glass
****

Fiery Hot Anus recipe

Description

A delicious recipe for Fiery Hot Anus, with Corona® lager, Bacardi® 151 rum and Tabasco® sauce.

Ingredients

12 oz bottle Corona® lager
3 oz Bacardi® 151 rum
Tabasco® sauce

Instructions

Pour the Bacardi 151 rum into a freshly opened bottle of Corona lager. Fill to the brim with Tabasco sauce. Serve cold, lime optional.

Serving

Bottle
****

Fire and Ice recipe

Description

A delicious recipe for Fire and Ice, with Bacardi® 151 rum and Goldschlager® cinnamon schnapps.

Ingredients

1/2 oz Bacardi® 151 rum
1/2 oz Goldschlager® cinnamon schnapps

Instructions

Pour both ingredients into a shot glass in equal parts,   and serve.

Serving

Shot Glass
****

Fireball Shooter recipe

Description

A delicious recipe for Fireball Shooter, with cinnamon schnapps, Bacardi® 151 rum and Tabasco® sauce.

Ingredients

1 shot cinnamon schnapps
1 shot Bacardi® 151 rum
2 dashes Tabasco® sauce

Instructions

Mix the schnapps, rum and tabasco in a shooter glass. Stir briefly.

Serving

Shot Glass
****

Firestorm recipe

Description

A delicious recipe for Firestorm, with cinnamon schnapps, peppermint schnapps and Bacardi® 151 rum.

Ingredients

3/4 oz red cinnamon schnapps
3/4 oz peppermint schnapps
3/4 oz Bacardi® 151 rum

Instructions

Pour ingredients into a stainless steel shaker over ice, and shake until completely cold. Strain into an old-fashioned glass, and serve.

Serving

Old-Fashioned Glass
****

Five Green Brothers recipe

Description

A delicious recipe for Five Green Brothers, with Bacardi® 151 rum, Blue Curacao liqueur, Malibu® coconut rum, Bud Light® lager and Mountain Dew® citrus soda.

Ingredients

5 oz Bacardi® 151 rum
2 oz Blue Curacao liqueur
2 oz Malibu® coconut rum
1 splash Bud Light® lager
Mountain Dew® citrus soda

Instructions

Pour the Bacardi 151, blue curacao and Malibu rum into a collins glass half-filled with ice cubes. Stir well. Fill with mountain dew, to taste. Stir briefly, and serve.

Serving

Collins Glass
****

Flaming Blue Jesus recipe

Description

A delicious recipe for Flaming Blue Jesus, with Bacardi® 151 rum, peppermint schnapps, Southern Comfort® peach liqueur and tequila.

Ingredients

1 oz Bacardi® 151 rum
1/2 oz peppermint schnapps
1/2 oz Southern Comfort® peach liqueur
1/2 oz tequila

Instructions

Layer with 151 proof rum on top. Light on fire - burn for 5 seconds - blow it out and drink.

Serving

Shot Glass
****

Flaming Blue recipe

Description

A delicious recipe for Flaming Blue, with anisette, vermouth and Bacardi® 151 rum.

Ingredients

1/2 oz anisette
1/2 oz vermouth
1 splash Bacardi® 151 rum

Instructions

Mix into a shot glass, and splash the bacardi on the very top. Be careful not to mix it into the rest of the drink. Then carefully light the rum on fire with a match. Blow   out the flame and drink it fast before the rim gets too hot.

Serving

Shot Glass
****

Flaming Citrus Action recipe

Description

A delicious recipe for Flaming Citrus Action, with Bacardi® Limon rum, Maui® tropical schnapps, orange juice and Tabasco® sauce.

Ingredients

1 part Bacardi® Limon rum
1 part Maui® tropical schnapps
2 parts orange juice
1 drop Tabasco® sauce

Instructions

Pour ingredients over ice in an ordinary glass.

Serving

Collins Glass
****

Flaming Cock Smack recipe

Description

A delicious recipe for Flaming Cock Smack, with dark rum, 99 Bananas® banana schnapps, peach schnapps, Bacardi® 151 rum and pineapple juice.

Ingredients

1 oz dark rum
1 oz 99 Bananas® banana schnapps
1/4 oz peach schnapps
1/4 oz Bacardi® 151 rum
12 oz pineapple juice

Instructions

Combine ice cubes with the pineapple juice, banana schnapps, and peach schnapps in a cocktail shaker and shake. Pour into a large collins glass then layer the Bacardi 151 on top with the back of a spoon. Ignite and allow to burn, extinguish and serve.

Serving

Collins Glass
****

Flaming Daniel recipe

Description

A delicious recipe for Flaming Daniel, with Bacardi® 151 rum, ouzo anise liqueur and absinthe herbal liqueur.

Ingredients

1 oz Bacardi® 151 rum
1 oz ouzo anise liqueur
1 oz absinthe herbal liqueur

Instructions

Combine ingredients together in an old-fashioned glass. Stir, ignite, and serve.

Serving

Old-Fashioned Glass
****

Flaming Dragon recipe

Description

A delicious recipe for Flaming Dragon, with Green Chartreuse® and Bacardi® 151 rum.

Ingredients

1 oz Green Chartreuse®
1 oz Bacardi® 151 rum

Instructions

Mix together. Light on fire. Let the flames warm the concoction for about 20 secs. Blow out fire (optional). Swallow quickly (take care).

****

Flaming Gay Morgan recipe

Description

A delicious recipe for Flaming Gay Morgan, with Captain Morgan® Original spiced rum, DeKuyper® Cheri-Beri Pucker schnapps, tonic water and Bacardi® 151 rum.

Ingredients

1 oz Captain Morgan® Original spiced rum
1 oz DeKuyper® Cheri-Beri Pucker schnapps
6 oz tonic water
1 dash Bacardi® 151 rum

Instructions

Pour the spiced rum, cherry liqueur and tonic water into a cocktail shaker half-filled with cracked ice. Shake well. Strain into a highball glass, and garnish with a slice of lime and a maraschino cherry. If desired, float the Bacardi 151 on top of the drink and ignite (use extreme caution). Extinguish before serving.

Serving

Highball Glass
****

Flaming Gorilla recipe

Description

A delicious recipe for Flaming Gorilla, with peppermint schnapps, Kahlua® coffee liqueur and Bacardi® 151 rum.

Ingredients

1 part peppermint schnapps
1 part Kahlua® coffee liqueur
1 part Bacardi® 151 rum

Instructions

Pour into shot glass, layering ingredients, from top to bottom. Light on fire and extinguish after 15 seconds.

Serving

Shot Glass
****

Flaming Gorilla Titties recipe

Description

A delicious recipe for Flaming Gorilla Titties, with Bacardi® 151 rum and Kahlua® coffee liqueur.

Ingredients

1 oz Bacardi® 151 rum
1 oz Kahlua® coffee liqueur

Instructions

Add the kahlua and then add bacardi 151 rum to the shot glass. Place a small sipping straw in the mixture and then light on fire. The straw is so you do not burn your eyebrows off. Once lit suck the shot through the straw till empty. Tastes like chocolate milk.

I have made this drink quite often at parties and it goes over very well with everyone. Try it a few times it does take a little practice to get it right.

Serving

Shot Glass

****

Flaming Hot Chocolate recipe

Description

A delicious recipe for Flaming Hot Chocolate, with dark creme de cacao and Bacardi® 151 rum.

Ingredients

3/4 oz dark creme de cacao
1/4 oz Bacardi® 151 rum

Instructions

Fill a shot glass three-quarters full with creme de cacao. Top with Bacardi 151 rum and ignite. Allow to burn for 10- 20 seconds, extinguish and serve.

Serving

Shot Glass
****

Flaming Jesus recipe

Description

A delicious recipe for Flaming Jesus, with Absolut® vodka, lime juice, grenadine syrup and Bacardi® 151 rum.

Ingredients

1 1/2 oz Absolut® vodka
1 splash lime juice
1 splash grenadine syrup
Bacardi® 151 rum

Instructions

Pour vodka, lime juice, and grenadine into shot glass. Then layer 151 proof rum on top from the back of a spoon. Light the 151 and shoot it while lit if you dare. If you are worried about shooting a lit drink, just blow out the flame and then shoot the drink.

Serving

Shot Glass
****

Flaming Jew recipe

Description

A delicious recipe for Flaming Jew, with Bacardi® 151 rum, Aftershock® Hot & Cool cinnamon schnapps, Goldschlager® cinnamon schnapps, Tabasco® sauce and dill juice.

Ingredients

2 oz Bacardi® 151 rum

2 oz Aftershock® Hot & Cool cinnamon schnapps

2 oz Goldschlager® cinnamon schnapps

1 dash Tabasco® sauce

1 splash dill juice

Instructions

Mix ingredients together in a beer mug. Ignite, and serve.

Serving

Beer Mug
****

Flaming Liquid Cocaine Blaster recipe

Description

A delicious recipe for Flaming Liquid Cocaine Blaster, with Bacardi® 151 rum, Jagermeister® herbal liqueur, Goldschlager® cinnamon schnapps and Red Bull® energy drink.

Ingredients

1/2 oz Bacardi® 151 rum

1/2 oz Jagermeister® herbal liqueur

1/2 oz Goldschlager® cinnamon schnapps

8 oz can Red Bull® energy drink

Instructions

Layer all three half shots on top of one another, making sure to float the 151 on top. Ignite; drop into a glass filled with red bull and pound it.

Serving

Old-Fashioned Glass
****

Flaming Nerd recipe

Description

A delicious recipe for Flaming Nerd, with Bacardi® 151 rum, Boo Koo® energy drink and orange juice.

Ingredients

1 oz Bacardi® 151 rum

1/2 oz Boo Koo® energy drink

1/2 oz orange juice

Instructions

Simply pour the ingredients into a double shot shot glass and serve.

Serving

Shot Glass
****

Flaming Orgasm recipe

Description

A delicious recipe for Flaming Orgasm, with beer and Bacardi® 151 rum.

Ingredients

12 oz beer
1 1/2 oz Bacardi® 151 rum

Instructions

Pour rum into a shot glass and the beer into a large mug. Light the rum on fire and drop into the beer. Make sure that the fire is out, then slam.

Serving

Beer Mug
****

Flaming Rasta recipe

Description

A delicious recipe for Flaming Rasta, with amaretto almond liqueur, grenadine syrup and Bacardi® 151 rum.

Ingredients

1 part amaretto almond liqueur
1 part grenadine syrup
1 part Bacardi® 151 rum

Instructions

Take a tall shot glass, a straw and a lighter. When the drink is poured make sure your 151 is on top. Take your straw and lick it so it is wet. Light the drink (run the lighter over top), put your straw in and drink it fast.

Serving

Shot Glass
****

Flaming Russian recipe

Description

A delicious recipe for Flaming Russian, with vodka and Bacardi® 151 rum.

Ingredients

1 oz vodka

1/5 oz Bacardi® 151 rum

Instructions

Pour vodka in shot glass, carefully layer rum on top. Ignite rum and serve.

Serving

Shot Glass
****

Flaming Spanish Fly recipe

Description

A delicious recipe for Flaming Spanish Fly, with Jose Cuervo® Especial gold tequila, Kahlua® coffee liqueur, Bacardi® 151 rum, coffee, whipped cream, sugar and cherry.

Ingredients

1 oz Jose Cuervo® Especial gold tequila
1 oz Kahlua® coffee liqueur
1 oz Bacardi® 151 rum
rich black coffee
1 1/2 oz whipped cream
coarse sugar
1 cherry

Instructions

Moisten rim of glass with cherry juice or water. Dip rim into coarse sugar to coat heavily. Pour tequila and coffee liquor into glass. Gently float 151 proof rum on top. Carefully ignite rum and swirl glass to lightly melt sugar with flame. Immediately pour in coffee to extinguish flames and fill cup. Top with whipped cream and cherry.

Serving

Irish Coffee Cup
****

Flaming Tiki Torch recipe

Description

A delicious recipe for Flaming Tiki Torch, with Malibu® coconut rum, peach schnapps, pineapple juice, DeKuyper® Razzmatazz liqueur, Smirnoff® Ice and Bacardi® 151 rum.

Ingredients

1/2 oz Malibu® coconut rum
1/4 oz peach schnapps
1 splash pineapple juice
1/4 oz DeKuyper® Razzmatazz liqueur
6 oz Smirnoff® Ice
1 splash Bacardi® 151 rum

Instructions

Place 2 highball glasses next to each other, one right side up, and one upside down. Stack a shot glass on on in between the two highball glasses.

Combine the Malibu rum, peach schnapps, and pineapple juice in a cocktail shaker half-filled with ice cubes, and shake well.

Fill the right side up tall glass half way with Smirnoff Ice. Pour the contents of your cocktail shaker into the shot glass. Add a splash of Razzmatazz and 151 to the shot glass.

Next step is optional; either light the top of the shot with a match, or blow fire at it with 151 in your mouth. Then, knock the shot glass into the tall glass and serve.

Serving

Highball Glass
****

Flatliner #2 recipe

Description

A delicious recipe for Flatliner #2, with Goldschlager® cinnamon schnapps, Grand Marnier® orange liqueur and Bacardi® 151 rum.

Ingredients

1 oz Goldschlager® cinnamon schnapps
1 oz Grand Marnier® orange liqueur
1 oz Bacardi® 151 rum

Instructions

Shake goldschlager and grand marnier well in a cocktail shaker with ice. Pour into a chilled cocktail/martini glass, top with bacardi 151 rum, and serve. (Can ignite rum if desired for optimal effect.)

Serving

Old-Fashioned Glass
****

Flying Grapefruit recipe

Description

A delicious recipe for Flying Grapefruit, with Bacardi® white rum, Martini & Rossi® dry vermouth, vodka, cranberry juice, lemon juice and grapefruit juice.

Ingredients

1 oz Bacardi® white rum
1/2 oz Martini & Rossi® dry vermouth
1/2 oz vodka

1 oz cranberry juice
1 oz fresh lemon juice
3 oz grapefruit juice

Instructions

Pour the rum, vodka, cranberry juice and lemon juice into a sugar-frosted highball glass almost filled with ice cubes. Stir well. Add the cranberry juice, then the vermouth, and serve.

Serving

Highball Glass
****

Four Horsemen #3 recipe

Description

A delicious recipe for Four Horsemen #3, with Jagermeister® herbal liqueur, Rumple Minze® peppermint liqueur, Bacardi® 151 rum and Goldschlager® cinnamon schnapps.

Ingredients

3/4 oz Jagermeister® herbal liqueur
3/4 oz pre-chilled Rumple Minze® peppermint liqueur
3/4 oz Bacardi® 151 rum
3/4 oz Goldschlager® cinnamon schnapps

Instructions

Pour contents into an old-fashioned glass, give a slight stir and serve.

Serving

Old-Fashioned Glass
****

Four Horsemen recipe

Description

A delicious recipe for Four Horsemen, with Jose Cuervo® Especial gold tequila, Jagermeister® herbal liqueur, Rumple Minze® peppermint liqueur and Bacardi® 151 rum.

Ingredients

3/4 oz Jose Cuervo® Especial gold tequila
3/4 oz Jagermeister® herbal liqueur
3/4 oz Rumple Minze® peppermint liqueur
3/4 oz Bacardi® 151 rum

Instructions

Pour contents in shaker over ice and shake well. Pour into glass. This is a big shooter so you have to use a small rocks glass.

Serving

Old-Fashioned Glass
****

Franko Ra recipe

Description

A delicious recipe for Franko Ra, with Bacardi® white rum, orange juice, lemon juice and sugar.

Ingredients

1 oz Bacardi® white rum
2/3 oz orange juice
1/3 oz lemon juice
1 tsp sugar

Instructions

Combine all ingredients in a cocktail shaker half-filled with ice cubes. Shake well, strain into a cocktail glass, and serve.

Serving

Cocktail Glass
****

Frozen O recipe

Description

A delicious recipe for Frozen O, with Bacardi® O rum, sugar and Kool-Aid® Orange mix.

Ingredients

1/2 cup Bacardi® O rum
1/2 cup sugar
1 package Kool-Aid® Orange mix

Instructions

Combine Kool-Aid orange mix, sugar, and Bacardi O orange rum in a blender with ice. Blend until smooth and frosty, pour into a tall glass and serve.

Serving

Hurricane Glass
****

Fruit Blast Martini Cocktail recipe

Description

A delicious recipe for Fruit Blast Martini Cocktail, with Bacardi® orange rum, Bacardi® Tropico rum, pineapple juice and cranberry juice.

Ingredients

1 oz Bacardi® orange rum
1 oz Bacardi® Tropico rum
1 1/2 oz pineapple juice
1 oz cranberry juice

Instructions

Shake ingredients with ice, strain into a martini glass and garnish with a strawberry.

Serving

Cocktail Glass
****

Fruit Lush recipe

Description

A delicious recipe for Fruit Lush, with Bacardi® light rum, peach schnapps, wildberry schnapps, creme de bananes, pineapple juice and Sprite® soda.

Ingredients

1 1/2 oz Bacardi® light rum
1 1/2 oz peach schnapps
1 1/2 oz wildberry schnapps
1/2 oz creme de bananes
2 1/2 oz pineapple juice
fill with Sprite® soda

Instructions

Mix ingredients in order, stir, enjoy.

Serving

Old-Fashioned Glass
****

Fruitopia recipe

Description

A delicious recipe for Fruitopia, with amaretto almond liqueur, Malibu® coconut rum, Bacardi® Limon rum, pineapple juice, orange juice and grenadine syrup.

Ingredients

1 shot amaretto almond liqueur
1 shot Malibu® coconut rum
1 shot Bacardi® Limon rum
1 oz pineapple juice
1 oz orange juice

1 dash grenadine syrup

Instructions

Pour ingredients, shake with ice and serve with a straw. Garnish with an orange slice if desired.

Serving

Hurricane Glass

****

Fruity as Fuck recipe

Description

A delicious recipe for Fruity as Fuck, with Bacardi® Razz rum, Stoli® Razberi vodka, Red Bull® energy drink, orange juice and cranberry juice.

Ingredients

1 1/2 oz Bacardi® Razz rum
1 1/2 oz Stoli® Razberi vodka
1 1/2 oz Red Bull® energy drink
1 1/2 oz orange juice
1 splash cranberry juice

Instructions

Pour the Bacardi Raz and Stolichnaya raspberry vodka (Stoli Razberi) followed by the orange juice and Red Bull into a highball glass. Splash with cranberry juice. Garnish with a slice of orange, with a cherry on a pick, and serve.

Serving

Highball Glass

****

Fruity Pebble #2 recipe

Description

A delicious recipe for Fruity Pebble #2, with Bacardi® Limon rum, lime juice and cranberry juice.

Ingredients

2 oz Bacardi® Limon rum
1 oz lime juice
5 - 6 oz cranberry juice

Instructions

Stir ingredients together in an old-fashioned or rocks glass filled with ice cubes, and serve.

Serving

Old-Fashioned Glass

Fu** Me Like A Beast recipe

Description

A delicious recipe for Fu** Me Like A Beast, with tequila, Midori® melon liqueur, Chambord® raspberry liqueur, pineapple juice, orange juice, grenadine syrup and Bacardi® 151 rum.

Ingredients

1/2 oz tequila
1/2 oz Midori® melon liqueur
1/2 oz Chambord® raspberry liqueur
1 part pineapple juice
1 part orange juice
1 dash grenadine syrup
top with Bacardi® 151 rum

Instructions

Combine all ingredients except 151, shake well with ice, pour into highball glass and top it off with bacardi 151.

Serving

Highball Glass

Fuck Me Over Again recipe

Description

A delicious recipe for Fuck Me Over Again, with triple sec, Bacardi® light rum, Montezuma® gold tequila, ginger ale and orange juice.

Ingredients

1 oz triple sec
1 oz Bacardi® light rum
1 oz Montezuma® gold tequila
2 oz ginger ale
3 oz orange juice

Instructions

Pour triple sec, light rum and tequila into a highball glass over ice. Stir together, then add orange juice and ginger ale. Serve.

Serving

Highball Glass

Fucked Up Motherfucker recipe

Description

A delicious recipe for Fucked Up Motherfucker, with Bacardi® 151 rum and Jagermeister® herbal liqueur.

Ingredients

1/2 oz Bacardi® 151 rum
1/2 oz Jagermeister® herbal liqueur

Instructions

Pour ingredients in equal parts into a shot glass, stir, and serve.

Serving

Shot Glass
****

Fuzzy Balls recipe

Description

A delicious recipe for Fuzzy Balls, with Absolut® Citron vodka, Bacardi® Limon rum, peach schnapps and 7-Up® soda.

Ingredients

1 part Absolut® Citron vodka
1 part Bacardi® Limon rum
1 part peach schnapps
fill with 7-Up® soda

Instructions

Mix alcoholic ingredients one part each - and add 7-up. Eight shots of each requires a 2L bottle of 7-up.

Serving

Punch Bowl
****

Fuzzy Bastard recipe

Description

A delicious recipe for Fuzzy Bastard, with Bacardi® dark rum, Bacardi® 151 rum, Orange Curacao liqueur, raspberry syrup, orange juice, sweet and sour mix and peach schnapps.

Ingredients

1 oz Bacardi® dark rum
1/2 oz Bacardi® 151 rum
1/2 oz Orange Curacao liqueur
1/2 oz raspberry syrup
fill with 1/2 orange juice
fill with 1/2 sweet and sour mix

1/2 oz peach schnapps

Instructions

Pour ingredients in order listed above into a Hurricane glass filled with ice.Garnish with an Orange Slice.

Serving

Hurricane Glass

****

Fuzzy Delight recipe

Description

A delicious recipe for Fuzzy Delight, with Arrow® peach schnapps, Bacardi® white rum and Sunny Delight® California Style orange juice.

Ingredients

1 oz Arrow® peach schnapps
1 oz Bacardi® white rum
5 oz Sunny Delight® California Style orange juice

Instructions

Pour Arrow peach schnapps into an ice-filled highball glass. Add Bacardi white rum, fill with Sunny Delight california style, and serve.

Serving

Highball Glass

****

Fuzzy Iron Worker recipe

Description

A delicious recipe for Fuzzy Iron Worker, with Captain Morgan® Original spiced rum, Bacardi® orange rum, Chambord® raspberry liqueur and pineapple juice.

Ingredients

1 oz Captain Morgan® Original spiced rum
1/2 oz Bacardi® orange rum
1/8 oz Chambord® raspberry liqueur
1 splash pineapple juice

Instructions

Shake all ingredients together in a cocktail shaker. Strain into a double-shot glass, and serve.

Serving

Shot Glass
****

Fuzzy Leprechaun recipe

Description

A delicious recipe for Fuzzy Leprechaun, with Bacardi® 151 rum and Gatorade® energy drink.

Ingredients

1 1/2 oz Bacardi® 151 rum
8 oz chilled Gatorade® energy drink

Instructions

Pour both ingredients into a highball glass, stir, and serve.

Serving

Highball Glass
****

Gator Piss recipe

Description

A delicious recipe for Gator Piss, with Bacardi® Limon rum, Midori® melon liqueur, sweet and sour mix and ice.

Ingredients

1 oz Bacardi® Limon rum
2 oz Midori® melon liqueur
fill with sweet and sour mix
ice

Instructions

Pour midori and rum over ice, and top off with sweet and sour mix.

Serving

Cocktail Glass
****

Gege recipe

Description

A delicious recipe for Gege, with Bacardi® Superior rum, creme de bananes and lemon juice.

Ingredients

3 cl Bacardi® Superior rum
1 cl creme de bananes
1 cl fresh lemon juice

Instructions

Shake ingredients and pour into a cocktail glass. Garnish with a red cherry, and serve.

Serving

Cocktail Glass
****

Get Faced recipe

Description

A delicious recipe for Get Faced, with Bacardi® 151 rum, Absolut® Citron vodka, gin and Coca-Cola®.

Ingredients

1 part Bacardi® 151 rum
1 part Absolut® Citron vodka
1 part gin
1 part Coca-Cola®

Instructions

Pour contents on ice pour into shaker give one hard shake then pour back into glass serve chilled

****

Go-Go Girl recipe

Description

A delicious recipe for Go-Go Girl, with Bacardi® light rum, mango nectar and pineapple juice.

Ingredients

1 1/2 oz Bacardi® light rum
1 1/2 oz mango nectar
3 1/2 oz pineapple juice

Instructions

Fill a highball glass with ice. Add rum and mango nectar. Top off glass with pineapple juice. Stir. Garnish with a slice of pineapple, and serve.

Serving

Highball Glass
****

Golden Cola recipe

Description

A delicious recipe for Golden Cola, with ice, Goldschlager® cinnamon schnapps, Bacardi® 151 rum, vanilla liqueur and Coca-Cola®.

Ingredients

1/2 glass ice
4 shots Goldschlager® cinnamon schnapps
1 shot Bacardi® 151 rum
1 shot vanilla liqueur
1 can Coca-Cola®

Instructions

Fill a highball glass halfway with crushed ice. Add alcohol contents over ice. Pour coke over mixture. Mix well.

Serving

Highball Glass
****

Golden Girl recipe

Description

A delicious recipe for Golden Girl, with Bacardi® 8 rum, simple syrup, pineapple juice, Offley Rich® tawny port and egg.

Ingredients

1 oz Bacardi® 8 rum
1/2 oz simple syrup
1 oz pineapple juice
3/4 oz Offley Rich® tawny port
1/2 egg

Instructions

SHake all ingredients well with ice and strain into a chilled martini glass. Garnish with grated orange zest, and serve.

Serving

Cocktail Glass
****

Golden Sunrise recipe

Description

A delicious recipe for Golden Sunrise, with amaretto almond liqueur, Bacardi® spiced rum, wildberry schnapps, DeKuyper® Key Largo schnapps, DeKuyper® Razzmatazz liqueur, orange juice and pineapple juice. Also lists similar drink re

Ingredients

1/4 oz amaretto almond liqueur
1/4 oz Bacardi® spiced rum
1/4 oz wildberry schnapps
1/4 oz DeKuyper® Key Largo schnapps
1/4 oz DeKuyper® Razzmatazz liqueur
1/2 part orange juice
1/2 part pineapple juice

Instructions

Pour amaretto, rum, and liqueurs into a mixing glass with/without ice. Top as desired with equal amounts of orange and pineapple juice, and shake well. Serve in a tall glass.

Serving

Hurricane Glass
****

Goombay Smash #3 recipe

Description

A delicious recipe for Goombay Smash #3, with Bacardi® gold rum, Bacardi® Coco rum, pineapple juice and sweet and sour mix.

Ingredients

1 oz Bacardi® gold rum
1 oz Bacardi® Coco rum
4 oz pineapple juice
1 splash sweet and sour mix

Instructions

Pour the Bacardi gold rum and Bacardi Coco rum, along with the pineapple juice into a cocktail shaker half-filled with ice cubes. Shake untill well chilled. Strain into a highball glass filled with ice cubes, and add a splash of sweet and sour mix. Stir lightly and serve.

Serving

Highball Glass
****

Goombay Smash Bahamas recipe

Description

A delicious recipe for Goombay Smash Bahamas, with Bacardi® light rum, coconut rum, pineapple juice, orange juice and grenadine syrup.

Ingredients

1 oz Bacardi® light rum
1 oz coconut rum

2 oz pineapple juice

2 oz orange juice

1 dash grenadine syrup

Instructions

Fill a hurricane glass with crushed (or cubed) ice. Add ingredients and stir. Garnish with an orange slice and a maraschino cherry, and serve. Frozen pineapple/orange concentrate made into juice can conveniently be used as a substitute for both juices combined.

Serving

Hurricane Glass

****

Goombay Smash Charleston Style recipe

Description

A delicious recipe for Goombay Smash Charleston Style, with Bacardi® white rum, Captain Morgan® Original spiced rum, banana, orange juice, pineapple juice and grenadine syrup.

Ingredients

1 oz Bacardi® white rum

3/4 oz Captain Morgan® Original spiced rum

1/3 fresh, sliced banana

2 oz orange juice

3 oz pineapple juice

1 splash grenadine syrup

Instructions

Cut banana into small pieces; mix with rums and juices and ice in a mixing tin; shake vigorously, pour into glass, and add a splash of grenadine for color.

Serving

Hurricane Glass

****

GordBuster from Hell recipe

Description

A delicious recipe for GordBuster from Hell, with vodka, Southern Comfort® peach liqueur, Bacardi® Razz rum, Captain Morgan® Original spiced rum and orange juice.

Ingredients

2 oz vodka

2 oz Southern Comfort® peach liqueur

2 oz Bacardi® Razz rum

2 oz Captain Morgan® Original spiced rum

4 oz orange juice

Instructions
Pour ingredients into a cocktail shaker half-filled with ice cubes. Shake well, pour into an old-fashioned or highball glass, and serve.

Serving
Highball Glass
****

Gorilla Cocktail recipe

Description
A delicious recipe for Gorilla Cocktail, with Bacardi® 151 rum and Jagermeister® herbal liqueur.

Ingredients
1 shot Bacardi® 151 rum
1 shot Jagermeister® herbal liqueur

Instructions
Add ingredients together and serve.

Serving
Old-Fashioned Glass
****

Gorilla Fart #5 recipe

Description
A delicious recipe for Gorilla Fart #5, with Bacardi® 151 rum and Yukon Jack® Canadian whisky.

Ingredients
1 oz Bacardi® 151 rum
1 oz Yukon Jack® Canadian whisky

Instructions
Pour yukon jack into a shot glass. Add the bacardi 151 proof rum.

Serving
Shot Glass
****

Gorilla Fart recipe

Description
A delicious recipe for Gorilla Fart, with Bacardi® 151   rum and Wild Turkey® 101 bourbon whiskey.

Ingredients

1/2 oz Bacardi® 151 rum
1/2 oz Wild Turkey® 101 bourbon whiskey

Instructions

Pour ingredients as listed above into a shot glass and shoot!

Serving

Shot Glass
****

Gorilla Smile recipe

Description

A delicious recipe for Gorilla Smile, with banana, strawberries, fruit punch, Bacardi® light rum, banana liqueur and peach schnapps.

Ingredients

1/2 banana
3 oz strawberries
2 oz fruit punch
2 oz Bacardi® light rum
1 oz banana liqueur
1 1/2 oz peach schnapps

Instructions

Combine all in a blender with 8-12 oz of ice, blend. Garnish with a banana slice speared through an umbrella.

Serving

Hurricane Glass
****

Grand Fashion recipe

Description

A delicious recipe for Grand Fashion, with sugar, cherry, orange, ice, Bacardi® white rum and red wine.

Ingredients

1 tsp sugar
1 cherry
1 orange
ice
Bacardi® white rum
red wine

Instructions

Muddle a teaspoon of sugar, cherry and orange in a chilled martini glass. Add ice, bacardi barrel aged rum, and rouge aperitif wine. Shake well. Garnish with a blood orange wheel.

Serving

Cocktail Glass
****

Gravedigger recipe

Description

A delicious recipe for Gravedigger, with Bacardi® 151 rum and Jim Beam® bourbon whiskey.

Ingredients

1/2 shot Bacardi® 151 rum
1/2 shot Jim Beam® bourbon whiskey

Instructions

Fill a shot glass half and half with bacardi 151 and jim beam whiskey in any order you want.

Serving

Shot Glass
****

Greazy Deigo recipe

Description

A delicious recipe for Greazy Deigo, with Zima, Bacardi® 151 rum and Kool-Aid® Mango mix.

Ingredients

12 oz Zima
2 shots Bacardi® 151 rum
Kool-Aid® Mango mix

Instructions

Empty zima into a glass. Add the bacardi, followed by the kool-aid. Mix until a light froth is achieved, and serve.

Serving

Collins Glass
****

Greek Sex On The Beach recipe

Description

A delicious recipe for Greek Sex On The Beach, with vodka, Bacardi® Limon rum, grenadine syrup, orange juice, gold tequila and Southern Comfort® peach liqueur.

Ingredients

2 parts vodka
1 1/2 parts Bacardi® Limon rum
2 parts grenadine syrup
2 1/2 parts orange juice
1 part gold tequila
1 part Southern Comfort® peach liqueur

Instructions

Put all ingredients in together, and shake. Serve in a glass filled up to 2/3 with ice.

Serving

Highball Glass
****

Green Demon #2 recipe

Description

A delicious recipe for Green Demon #2, with Bacardi® Limon rum and Hawaiian punch.

Ingredients

4 oz Bacardi® Limon rum
8 oz green Hawaiian punch

Instructions

Pour the Bacardi Limon into a highball glass. Add green hawaiian punch. Stir well, and serve.

Serving

Highball Glass
****

Green Mamba recipe

Description

A delicious recipe for Green Mamba, with Midori® melon liqueur, sweet and sour mix, club soda and Bacardi® 151 rum.

Ingredients

1 oz Midori® melon liqueur
2 oz sweet and sour mix
2 oz club soda
1 oz Bacardi® 151 rum

Instructions

Fill a hurricane glass with ice. Add the Midori melon liqueur then equal amounts of sweet and sour mix and club soda. Top with Bacardi 151, and serve.

Green Monster #2 recipe

Description

A delicious recipe for Green Monster #2, with Bacardi® 151 rum, lime juice, food coloring and ice cubes.

Ingredients

1 oz Bacardi® 151 rum
1/2 oz lime juice
3 dashes green food coloring
4 ice cubes

Instructions

Pour 151 rum, lime juice, and food coloring into a glass with several ice cubes. Shake, and strain into a shot glass.

Serving

Shot Glass
****

Green Motherfucker recipe

Description

A delicious recipe for Green Motherfucker, with Bacardi® 151 rum and green creme de menthe.

Ingredients

1/2 oz Bacardi® 151 rum
1/2 oz green creme de menthe

Instructions

Pour each ingredient into a shot glass.

Serving

Shot Glass
****

Green Spider recipe

Description

A delicious recipe for Green Spider, with Bacardi® 151 rum and green creme de menthe.

Ingredients

1 shot Bacardi® 151 rum
1/2 shot green creme de menthe

Instructions

Add the bacardi 151 to a shot glass, then add creme de menthe.

Serving

Shot Glass
****

Grim Reaper recipe

Description

A delicious recipe for Grim Reaper, with Kahlua® coffee liqueur, Bacardi® 151 rum and grenadine syrup.

Ingredients

1 oz Kahlua® coffee liqueur
1 oz Bacardi® 151 rum
1 dash grenadine syrup

Instructions

Mix kahlua and 151 proof rum in an old-fashioned glass. Quickly add ice and pour grenadine over the top to give an ice red tint.

Serving

Old-Fashioned Glass
****

Guilty Verdict recipe

Description

A delicious recipe for Guilty Verdict, with Bacardi® 151 rum and orange juice.

Ingredients

1 oz Bacardi® 151 rum
6 oz orange juice

Instructions

Pour Bacardi 151 into a highball glass half-filled with ice. Add orange juice, and serve.

Serving

Highball Glass
****

Gulyuz recipe

Description

A delicious recipe for Gulyuz, with Bacardi® light rum, Safari® liqueur, Blue Curacao liqueur and pineapple juice.

Ingredients

6 cl Bacardi® light rum
3 cl Safari® liqueur
2 cl Blue Curacao liqueur
fill with pineapple juice

Instructions

Pour all ingredients into a shaker half-filled with cracked ice and shake for 1 minute. Strain into a cocktail glass.

Serving

Cocktail Glass
****

Gumdrop Martini recipe

Description

A delicious recipe for Gumdrop Martini, with Bacardi® Limon rum, vodka, Southern Comfort® peach liqueur, dry vermouth and lemon juice.

Ingredients

2 oz Bacardi® Limon rum
1 oz vodka
1/2 oz Southern Comfort® peach liqueur
1/2 tsp dry vermouth
1/2 oz fresh lemon juice

Instructions

Pour all ingredients into a cocktail shaker half-filled with cracked ice. Shake well. Strain into a sugar-rimmed chilled cocktail glass. Garnish with a slice of lemon and some gumdrops, and serve.

Serving

Cocktail Glass
****

Hard Core recipe

Description

A delicious recipe for Hard Core, with Bacardi® 151 rum, Everclear® alcohol, triple sec, amaretto almond liqueur, Pepsi® cola and orange.

Ingredients

1 shot Bacardi® 151 rum
1 shot Everclear® alcohol
3/4 shot triple sec
3/4 shot amaretto almond liqueur
Pepsi® cola

1 orange wedge

Instructions

Combine all ingredients in a tall glass or wine goblet. Add the cola last. Hang orange on rim of glass.

Serving

Wine Goblet
****

Haywire recipe

Description

A delicious recipe for Haywire, with Bacardi® Limon rum and 7-Up® cherry soda.

Ingredients

1 part Bacardi® Limon rum
3 - 5 parts 7-Up® cherry soda

Instructions

Serve over ice. Regular 7-up and amaretto can be used if cherry 7-Up is not available. Garnish with an orange slice and cherry. Serve with a straw.

Serving

Collins Glass
****

Hell on Earth recipe

Description

A delicious recipe for Hell on Earth, with Bacardi® 151 rum and lemonade.

Ingredients

3 oz Bacardi® 151 rum
3 oz lemonade

Instructions

Pour both ingredients into a highball glass filled with ice cubes. Stir well, and serve.

Serving

Highball Glass
****

Hemingway Hammer recipe

Description

A delicious recipe for Hemingway Hammer, with Bacardi® 151 rum, Bacardi® white rum, blackberry brandy, strawberry liqueur and banana liqueur.

Ingredients

1 oz Bacardi® 151 rum
1 oz Bacardi® white rum
1 oz blackberry brandy
1 oz strawberry liqueur
1 oz banana liqueur

Instructions

Combine all ingredients with one cup of crushed ice in a cocktail shaker or blender for 30 seconds. Pour into a highball glass and serve with a lime wedge.

Serving

Highball Glass
****

Hobble Gobble recipe

Description

A delicious recipe for Hobble Gobble, with Wild Turkey® bourbon whiskey and Bacardi® 151 rum.

Ingredients

1/2 oz Wild Turkey® bourbon whiskey
1/2 oz Bacardi® 151 rum

Instructions

Pour Wild Turkey into a shot glass. Add Bacardi 151 proof rum, stir briefly and serve.

Serving

Shot Glass
****

Hokey Pokey recipe

Description

A delicious recipe for Hokey Pokey, with Bacardi® Razz rum, Bacardi® O rum, Bacardi® Limon rum, Malibu® coconut rum and pineapple juice.

Ingredients

1 oz Bacardi® Razz rum
1 oz Bacardi® O rum
1 oz Bacardi® Limon rum
1 oz Malibu® coconut rum
top with pineapple juice

Instructions

Combine all ingredients together in a cocktail shaker half-filled with ice cubes. Shake well, strain into shot glasses, and serve.

Serving

Shot Glass
****

Holiday Hangover recipe

Description

A delicious recipe for Holiday Hangover, with Bacardi® white rum and 7-Up® soda.

Ingredients

4 oz Bacardi® white rum
5 oz 7-Up® soda

Instructions

Stir ingredients together in a highball glass. Garnish with a candy cane, and serve.

Serving

Highball Glass
****

Hot Apple Pie with Sparks recipe

Description

A delicious recipe for Hot Apple Pie with Sparks, with Irish cream, Goldschlager® cinnamon schnapps, Bacardi® 151 rum and cinnamon.

Ingredients

1/2 oz Irish cream
1/2 oz Goldschlager® cinnamon schnapps
1 splash Bacardi® 151 rum
2 - 3 pinches cinnamon powder

Instructions

Layer the Irish cream and Goldschlager cinnamon schnapps in a shot glass. Very gently, pour the Bacardi 151 on top. Carefully ignite the 151. Throw small handfuls of cinnamon powder on top 2 - 3 times to make sparks. Blow out and serve.

Serving

Shot Glass
****

Hot Chicana recipe

Description

A delicious recipe for Hot Chicana, with Bacardi® white rum, DeKuyper® Hot Damn cinnamon schnapps and Tabasco® sauce.

Ingredients

1/2 oz Bacardi® white rum
1/2 oz DeKuyper® Hot Damn cinnamon schnapps
4 drops Tabasco® sauce

Instructions

Pour the Bacardi rum, DeKuyper Hot Damn cinnamon schnapps and Tabasco sauce into shot glass. Stir and serve.

Serving

Shot Glass
****

Hot Lunch recipe

Description

A delicious recipe for Hot Lunch, with Bacardi® 151 rum and Tabasco® sauce.

Ingredients

2 oz Bacardi® 151 rum
1 dash Tabasco® sauce

Instructions

Mix all ingredients in a cocktail glass. Garnish with a small pickle. Light contents of glass on fire. Tilt head back and have your buddy pour it into your mouth (very carefully). Have four more hot lunches and go to bed. You have no business going anywhere after the abuse you just gave yourself.

Serving

Cocktail Glass
****

Hot Mess recipe

Description

A delicious recipe for Hot Mess, with Bacardi® 151 rum, caramel syrup and Goldschlager® cinnamon schnapps.

Ingredients

1/2 oz Bacardi® 151 rum
1/4 oz caramel syrup
1/4 oz Goldschlager® cinnamon schnapps

Instructions

Carefully layer ingredients into a shot glass in this

order: Goldschlager bottom, Bacardi 151 middle, Caramel top.

For the Caramel, heat in a microwave to the point where its almost liquid. And add to the shot. Light the shot on fire, blow out flames and serve.

Serving

Shot Glass
****

Hurricane Laura recipe

Description

A delicious recipe for Hurricane Laura, with Bacardi® dark rum, passion-fruit juice, grenadine syrup and orange juice.

Ingredients

1 oz Bacardi® dark rum
1 oz passion-fruit juice
1/2 oz grenadine syrup
1/2 oz orange juice

Instructions

Stir and pour in shot glasses.

Serving

Shot Glass
****

Hurricane recipe

Description

A delicious recipe for Hurricane, with vodka, grenadine syrup, gin, light rum, Bacardi® 151 rum, amaretto almond liqueur, triple sec, grapefruit juice and pineapple juice.

Ingredients

1 oz vodka
1/4 oz grenadine syrup
1 oz gin
1 oz light rum
1/2 oz Bacardi® 151 rum
1 oz amaretto almond liqueur
1 oz triple sec
grapefruit juice
pineapple juice

Instructions

Pour all but the juices, in order listed, into a hurricane glass three-quarters filled with ice. Fill with equal parts of grapefruit and pineapple juice, and serve.

Serving

Hurricane Glass
****

Hurricane Sunrise recipe

Description

A delicious recipe for Hurricane Sunrise, with Bacardi® white rum, Bacardi® dark rum, Jose Cuervo® Especial gold tequila, orange juice, pineapple juice and grenadine syrup.

Ingredients

1 1/2 oz Bacardi® white rum
1 1/2 oz Bacardi® dark rum
2 oz Jose Cuervo® Especial gold tequila
4 - 8 oz orange juice
4 oz unsweetened pineapple juice
1 - 2 oz grenadine syrup

Instructions

Combine all ingredients in a hurricane glass with ice as desired, and mix well. Garnish with maraschino cherries and orange slices (optional), and serve.

Serving

Hurricane Glass
****

Hurricane, New Orleans Style recipe

Description

A delicious recipe for Hurricane, New Orleans Style, with white rum, Jamaican dark rum, Bacardi® 151 rum, orange juice, pineapple juice, grenadine syrup and crushed ice.

Ingredients

1 oz white rum
1 oz Jamaican dark rum
1 oz Bacardi® 151 rum
3 oz orange juice
3 oz unsweetened pineapple juice
1/2 oz grenadine syrup
crushed ice

Instructions

Combine all ingredients, mix well (shake or stir). Pour over crushed ice in hurricane glass. Best enjoyed through a small straw. Garnish with fruit wedge if desired.

Serving

Hurricane Glass
****

I See Dead People recipe

Description

A delicious recipe for I See Dead People, with Everclear® alcohol, Bacardi® 151 rum, Grey Goose® vodka and Wild Turkey® 101 bourbon whiskey.

Ingredients

1/2 oz Everclear® alcohol
1/2 oz Bacardi® 151 rum
1/2 oz Grey Goose® vodka
1/2 oz Wild Turkey® 101 bourbon whiskey

Instructions

Serve in equal parts in a 2-oz shot glass.

Serving

Shot Glass
****

Ichabod Crane recipe

Description

A delicious recipe for Ichabod Crane, with Bols® Pumpkin Smash liqueur, Frangelico® hazelnut liqueur, Bacardi® 151 rum and vanilla ice cream.

Ingredients

1 1/2 oz Bols® Pumpkin Smash liqueur
1 oz Frangelico® hazelnut liqueur
1/2 oz Bacardi® 151 rum
2 scoops vanilla ice cream

Instructions

Blend the ice cream with the Bols Pumpkin Smash and Frangelico hazelnut liqueur in a blender. Blend well and pour into a Champagne flute. Pour Bacardi 151 rum over the top and garnish with nutmeg or cinnamon.

Serving

Champagne Flute
****

IED (Improvised Explosive Device) recipe

Description

A delicious recipe for IED (Improvised Explosive Device), with Bacardi® 151 rum, Jagermeister® herbal liqueur, Goldschlager® cinnamon schnapps and Jose Cuervo® 1800 tequila.

Ingredients

1 shot Bacardi® 151 rum
1 shot Jagermeister® herbal liqueur
1 shot Goldschlager® cinnamon schnapps
1 shot Jose Cuervo® 1800 tequila

Instructions

Combine Jagermeister (smoke), Goldschlager (fragmentation), and Jose Cuervo tequila (because we had 1 Mexican in the platoon) in a highball or old-fashioned glass. After all ingredients have been combined drop some lit Bacardi 151 rum into the glass and shoot. After a couple of seconds when the intital shock has wore off you yell BAM!!

Serving

Highball Glass
****

Illusions recipe

Description

A delicious recipe for Illusions, with vodka, Bacardi® white rum, Midori® melon liqueur, Blue Curacao liqueur and orange juice.

Ingredients

1 part vodka
1 part Bacardi® white rum
1 part Midori® melon liqueur
2 parts Blue Curacao liqueur
orange juice

Instructions

Add all ingredients and fill the rest of the shaker with Orange Juice. Add ice and shake.

****

Indian Summer Cocktail recipe

Description

A delicious recipe for Indian Summer Cocktail, with Bacardi® white rum, Appleton Estate® Dark Jamaica rum, pineapple juice, grapefruit juice, currant syrup and Sprite® soda.

Ingredients

1 oz Bacardi® white rum
1 oz Appleton Estate® Dark Jamaica rum
2 oz pineapple juice
1 oz grapefruit juice
1/2 oz currant syrup
1 splash Sprite® soda

Instructions

Pour all ingredients into a highball glass filled with ice cubes, stir and serve.

Serving

Highball Glass
****

Instant Death recipe

Description

A delicious recipe for Instant Death, with Bacardi® 151 rum, Everclear® alcohol, Jagermeister® herbal liqueur, water and salt.

Ingredients

3 oz Bacardi® 151 rum
3 oz Everclear® alcohol
3 oz Jagermeister® herbal liqueur
5 oz water
1 dash salt

Instructions

Put in all alcoholic ingredients first, water last, then salt.

****

Irish Rootbeer recipe

Description

A delicious recipe for Irish Rootbeer, with Kahlua® coffee liqueur, amaretto almond liqueur, Bacardi® 151 rum and Guinness® stout.

Ingredients

1/2 oz Kahlua® coffee liqueur
1/2 oz amaretto almond liqueur
1 splash Bacardi® 151 rum

1/2 pint Guinness® stout

Instructions

Fill a shot glass half with Kahlua, half with amaretto, and a splash of Bacardi 151 rum. Drop it into a pint of Guinness, and serve.

Serving

Beer Mug
****

Irish Whip recipe

Description

A delicious recipe for Irish Whip, with vodka, Pernod® licorice liqueur, Bacardi® 151 rum, green creme de menthe, 7-Up® soda and orange juice.

Ingredients

1 oz vodka
1 oz Pernod® licorice liqueur
1 oz Bacardi® 151 rum
1 oz green creme de menthe
1 part 7-Up® soda
1 part orange juice

Instructions

Mix vodka, pernod, rum and creme de menthe together with a few ice cubes in a pint glass. Fill with equal parts of 7-up and orange juice, stir, and serve.

Serving

Beer Mug
****

Ironlung recipe

Description

A delicious recipe for Ironlung, with Yukon Jack® Canadian whisky, Bacardi® 151 rum and whipped cream.

Ingredients

1 oz Yukon Jack® Canadian whisky
3 drops Bacardi® 151 rum
1 1/2 oz whipped cream

Instructions

Pour yukon jack into a shot glass. Top with a small float of bacardi 151 rum. Add a small topping of whipped cream.

Serving

Shot Glass
****

Island Tide recipe

Description

A delicious recipe for Island Tide, with anejo rum, Bacardi® Limon rum, peach juice and lemon juice.

Ingredients

3 shots anejo rum
1 shot Bacardi® Limon rum
peach juice
1 - 2 splashes lemon juice

Instructions

Pour anejo rum and bacardi limon into a collins glass; with ice if desired. Almost fill with peach juice, and add lemon juice. Stir, and sink 3 mandarin orange and 2 peach slices to the bottom. Garnish the glass with a lemon slice, peach slice or mandarin orange slice if desired, and serve.

Serving

Collins Glass
****

Jake-Knife recipe

Description

A delicious recipe for Jake-Knife, with Jagermeister® herbal liqueur, Coca-Cola® and Bacardi® 151 rum.

Ingredients

2 oz Jagermeister® herbal liqueur
Coca-Cola®
1 dash Bacardi® 151 rum

Instructions

Pour jagermeister over ice in a cocktail shaker. Fill with coke, shake vigorously, and pour into a cocktail glass. Top with rum, and ignite if desired. Extinguish, and serve.

Serving

Cocktail Glass
****

Jamaican Ass-Kicker recipe

Description

A delicious recipe for Jamaican Ass-Kicker, with   Bacardi® 151 rum and Jolt® cola.

Ingredients

2 oz Bacardi® 151 rum
6 oz chilled Jolt® cola

Instructions

Pour in the rum. Top with cola.

Serving

Highball Glass
****

Jamaican Green Sunrise recipe

Description

A delicious recipe for Jamaican Green Sunrise, with Bacardi® white rum, orange juice, Blue Curacao liqueur, Finlandia® pineapple vodka and ice.

Ingredients

4 cl Bacardi® white rum
fill with orange juice
2 cl Blue Curacao liqueur
2 cl Finlandia® pineapple vodka
ice

Instructions

Start with the ice cubes. Pour rum and orange juice. Carefully add blue curacao, making sure it falls to the bottom. Layer pineapple vodka on top.

Serving

Cocktail Glass
****

Jamaican Me Crazy recipe

Description

A delicious recipe for Jamaican Me Crazy, with Bacardi® white rum, Malibu® coconut rum, banana liqueur, cranberry juice and pineapple juice.

Ingredients

1 oz Bacardi® white rum
1 oz Malibu® coconut rum
1 oz banana liqueur
1 splash cranberry juice
1 splash pineapple juice

Instructions

Mix in a shaker glass and serve.

Serving

Collins Glass
****

James D recipe

Description

A delicious recipe for James D, with Fanta® orange soda, Sprite® soda and Bacardi® Limon rum.

Ingredients

4 oz Fanta® orange soda
4 oz Sprite® soda
4 oz Bacardi® Limon rum

Instructions

Combine ingredients. Stir.

Serving

Collins Glass
****

Jello Love recipe

Description

A delicious recipe for Jello Love, with Bacardi® orange rum, DeKuyper® Watermelon Pucker schnapps, Cruzan® orange rum and Gatorade® Fierce Melon energy drink.

Ingredients

1 oz Bacardi® orange rum
1 1/2 oz DeKuyper® Watermelon Pucker schnapps
1 oz Cruzan® orange rum
6 oz Gatorade® Fierce Melon energy drink

Instructions

Pour the Bacardi O, DeKuyper Watermelon Pucker schnapps and Cruzan orange rum into a cup and mix well. Add the Gatorade Fierce Melon; do not stir. Chill for one hour before serving.

Serving

Cup
****

Jelly Donut recipe

Description

A delicious recipe for Jelly Donut, with Tropicana Twister Kinetic Kiwi Strawberry, Bacardi® white rum, DeKuyper® Razzmatazz liqueur and half-and-half.

Ingredients

4 1/2 oz Tropicana Twister Kinetic Kiwi Strawberry
3 oz Bacardi® white rum
1 1/2 oz DeKuyper® Razzmatazz liqueur
1 oz half-and-half

Instructions

Pour the Tropicana kiwi-strawberry juice, the Bacardi white rum, and the DeKuyper razzmatazz liqueur into a highball glass half-filled with ice cubes. Float about 1/2 inch of half-and-half onto the mixture; done by slowly pouring the cream over the back of a spoon so that the cream stays separate from the rest of the drink. Serve.

Serving

Highball Glass
****

Jens Special recipe

Description

A delicious recipe for Jens Special, with Bacardi® Limon rum, Sprite® soda and Red Bull® energy drink.

Ingredients

6 cl Bacardi® Limon rum
8 cl Sprite® soda
12 cl Red Bull® energy drink

Instructions

Pour bacardi lim?n into a glass, add the sprite and the red bull, then stir to mix.

Serving

Champagne Saucer
****

Jersey Cherry recipe

Description

A delicious recipe for Jersey Cherry, with Bacardi® white rum, cherry brandy and cola.

Ingredients

1 1/2 oz Bacardi® white rum
1 oz cherry brandy
fill with cola

Instructions

Build over ice in a rocks glass. Garnish with a cherry.

Serving

Old-Fashioned Glass
****

Jet Pilot recipe

Description

A delicious recipe for Jet Pilot, with spiced rum, Malibu® coconut rum, Bacardi® white rum, Bacardi® Limon rum, cranberry juice, orange juice, pineapple juice, grenadine syrup and Southern Comfort® peach liqueur. Also lists

Ingredients

1 oz spiced rum
1 oz Malibu® coconut rum
1 oz Bacardi® white rum
1 oz Bacardi® Limon rum
2 oz cranberry juice
2 oz orange juice
2 oz pineapple juice
1 tsp grenadine syrup
2 oz Southern Comfort® peach liqueur

Instructions

Add ice cubes to a mason jar glass. Pour in the rums, followed by the juices. Add the grenadine. Top with a double shot of southern comfort. More juice could be used to mask liquor. Drink can be stirred if preferred.

Serving

Mason Jar
****

Jim the Destroyer recipe

Description

A delicious recipe for Jim the Destroyer, with Jim Beam® bourbon whiskey, Bacardi® 151 rum, Chivas Regal® Scotch whisky and Jose Cuervo® Especial gold tequila.

Ingredients

1/2 oz Jim Beam® bourbon whiskey
1/2 oz Bacardi® 151 rum
1/2 oz Chivas Regal® Scotch whisky
1/2 oz Jose Cuervo® Especial gold tequila

Instructions

Stir ingredients together in a double-shot glass, and   serve.

Joe Cassano recipe

Description

A delicious recipe for Joe Cassano, with Zima, Absolut® Citron vodka, gin, Bacardi® 151 rum and lemonade.

Ingredients

1 oz Zima
1/2 oz Absolut® Citron vodka
1/2 oz gin
1/3 oz Bacardi® 151 rum
1 1/2 oz lemonade

Instructions

Combine ingredients with 1 oz of crushed ice in a blender. Pour into a chilled cocktail glass, top with lemonade (to taste), and serve.

Serving

Cocktail Glass
****

Jubilee on the Square recipe

Description

A delicious recipe for Jubilee on the Square, with Bacardi® white rum, Malibu® coconut rum, Midori® melon liqueur, pineapple juice and orange juice.

Ingredients

1 oz Bacardi® white rum
1 oz Malibu® coconut rum
1 oz Midori® melon liqueur
1 1/2 oz pineapple juice
1 1/2 oz orange juice

Instructions

Pour the Bacardi white rum, Malibu coconut rum, Midori melon liqueur, pineapple juice and orange juice into a cocktail shaker half-filled with ice cubes. Shake well, and strain into a highball glass filled with ice cubes. Garnish with a slice of orange, a pineapple wedge and a maraschino cherry. Serve.

Serving

Highball Glass
****

Kab-z Vanilla recipe

Description

A delicious recipe for Kab-z Vanilla, with Bacardi® Vanil rum, Pepsi® Vanilla cola, lime juice and lemon juice.

Ingredients

1 1/2 oz Bacardi® Vanil rum
4 oz Pepsi® Vanilla cola
1 drop lime juice
2 drops lemon juice

Instructions

Pour the Bacardi Vanil rum into an old-fashioned glass half-filled with crushed ice. Add the Pepsi vanilla cola and lime juice. Stir well. Add the lemon juice, and serve.

Serving

Old-Fashioned Glass
****

Kavorkien recipe

Description

A delicious recipe for Kavorkien, with Bacardi® spiced rum, Bacardi® black rum, Captain Morgan® Parrot Bay coconut rum, creme de noyaux, orange juice and cranberry juice.

Ingredients

1/2 oz Bacardi® spiced rum
1/2 oz Bacardi® black rum
1/2 oz Captain Morgan® Parrot Bay coconut rum
1/2 oz creme de noyaux
3/4 oz orange juice
3/4 oz cranberry juice

Instructions

Combine all ingredients into a mixing tin with ice. Shake and strain. Can be served over ice or up.

Serving

Whiskey Sour Glass
****

Keremiki recipe

Description

A delicious recipe for Keremiki, with Bacardi® 151 rum, Goldschlager® cinnamon schnapps and Rumple Minze® peppermint liqueur.

Ingredients

1/3 oz Bacardi® 151 rum
1/3 oz Goldschlager® cinnamon schnapps
1/3 oz Rumple Minze® peppermint liqueur

Instructions

Mix and shoot.

****

Kermit recipe

Description

A delicious recipe for Kermit, with Bacardi® white rum, Pisang Ambon® liqueur, Blue Curacao liqueur and banana liqueur.

Ingredients

1 1/2 cl Bacardi® white rum
1 1/2 cl Pisang Ambon® liqueur
1 1/2 cl Blue Curacao liqueur
1 1/2 cl banana liqueur

Instructions

Add ice and shake. Top up with orange juice.

Serving

Highball Glass
****

Kevin on the Floor recipe

Description

A delicious recipe for Kevin on the Floor, with Bacardi® 151 rum, Malibu® coconut rum and pineapple juice.

Ingredients

3 oz Bacardi® 151 rum
2 oz Malibu® coconut rum
8 oz chilled pineapple juice

Instructions

Pour the rums over some crushed ice in a tall collins glass. Fill with pineapple juice, and serve.

Serving

Collins Glass
****

Key Largo Kooler recipe

Description

A delicious recipe for Key Largo Kooler, with DeKuyper® Key Largo schnapps, Captain Morgan® Original spiced rum, orange juice, pineapple juice, cranberry juice and Bacardi® 151 rum.

Ingredients

1 oz DeKuyper® Key Largo schnapps
1/2 oz Captain Morgan® Original spiced rum
4 oz orange juice
4 oz pineapple juice
2 oz cranberry juice
1/2 oz Bacardi® 151 rum

Instructions

Mix juices and alcohol in a mixing tin, flash blend, and pour over ice in a 23 oz. squall glass and float bacardi 151 rum. Garnish with an orange flag and umbrella.

Serving

Hurricane Glass
****

Klukwan recipe

Description

A delicious recipe for Klukwan, with Bacardi® Razz rum and Sprite® soda.

Ingredients

3 oz Bacardi® Razz rum
3 oz Sprite® soda

Instructions

Mix Bacardi Razz with Sprite over ice cubes in a highball glass, and serve.

Serving

Highball Glass
****

Kryptonite Kooler recipe

Description

A delicious recipe for Kryptonite Kooler, with Bacardi® white rum, Maui® Blue Hawaiian schnapps and pineapple juice.

Ingredients

1 1/2 oz Bacardi® white rum
3 oz Maui® Blue Hawaiian schnapps
6 oz pineapple juice

Instructions

Mix the rum, maui, and pineapple juice together. Add ice, and enjoy.

Serving

Collins Glass
****

Kryptonite recipe

Description

A delicious recipe for Kryptonite, with Captain Morgan® Original spiced rum, Malibu® coconut rum, Midori® melon liqueur, pineapple juice and Bacardi® 151 rum.

Ingredients

3/4 oz Captain Morgan® Original spiced rum
3/4 oz Malibu® coconut rum
3/4 oz Midori® melon liqueur
3/4 oz pineapple juice
1 splash Bacardi® 151 rum

Instructions

Combine ingredients with ice in a cocktail shaker. Shake and strain into a cocktail glass, and serve.

Serving

Cocktail Glass
****

Kula-for-Shula recipe

Description

A delicious recipe for Kula-for-Shula, with Bacardi® 151 rum, vodka, Gatorade® Citrus Cooler energy drink and amaretto almond liqueur.

Ingredients

1/2 oz Bacardi® 151 rum
1 oz vodka
7 oz Gatorade® Citrus Cooler energy drink
1 splash amaretto almond liqueur

Instructions

Combine the Bacardi 151 rum, vodka, and Gatorade Citrus Cooler together over ice in a collins glass, and stir.

Finish with a splash of amaretto almond liqueur, and serve.

Serving

Collins Glass
****

La Pussy recipe

Description

A delicious recipe for La Pussy, with Bacardi® white rum, Cointreau® orange liqueur, brandy and DeKuyper® Apple Barrel schnapps.

Ingredients

1/3 oz Bacardi® white rum
1/3 oz Cointreau® orange liqueur
1/3 oz brandy
3 dashes DeKuyper® Apple Barrel schnapps

Instructions

Shake all ingredients with ice cubes, strain into a cocktail glass, and serve.

Serving

Cocktail Glass
****

Lake George Iced Tea recipe

Description

A delicious recipe for Lake George Iced Tea, with Jose Cuervo® Especial gold tequila, Bacardi® white rum, Absolut® vodka, Beefeater® gin, triple sec, pineapple juice and Pepsi® cola. Also lists similar drink recipes

Ingredients

1/2 oz Jose Cuervo® Especial gold tequila
1/2 oz Bacardi® white rum
1/2 oz Absolut® vodka
1/2 oz Beefeater® gin
1/2 oz triple sec
1 oz pineapple juice
Pepsi® cola

Instructions

Shake all ingredients (except cola), and pour into a highball glass. Fill with pepsi, stir gently, and serve.

Serving

Highball Glass
****

Lava Lamp recipe

Description

A delicious recipe for Lava Lamp, with DeKuyper® Raspberry Pucker schnapps, Bacardi® silver rum and Guinness® stout.

Ingredients

1 oz DeKuyper® Raspberry Pucker schnapps
1 oz Bacardi® silver rum
Guinness® stout

Instructions

Pour a shot of DeKuyper raspberry pucker schnapps into a shot glass. Place the shot glass inside the bottom of a pint glass. Pour Bacardi silver rum around the outside of shot glass (but inside the pint glass) and carefully float some on top of the raspberry pucker by pouring over the back of a spoon pressed against the inside of the shot glass. Top it all off with Guinness. If done correctly, all ingredients should stay separated until the drink is downed in one fell swoop.

Serving

Beer Mug
****

Lemon Celebration recipe

Description

A delicious recipe for Lemon Celebration, with Chambord® raspberry liqueur, Bacardi® Limon rum and Champagne.

Ingredients

1 oz Chambord® raspberry liqueur
1 oz Bacardi® Limon rum
3 oz Champagne

Instructions

Shake gently with ice (the champagne will fizz). Strain into a martini glass.

Serving

Cocktail Glass
****

Lemon Drop #7 recipe

Description

A delicious recipe for Lemon Drop #7, with Bacardi® Limon rum and lemonade.

Ingredients

1 part Bacardi® Limon rum
1 part lemonade

Instructions

Fill a mug half way with bacardi, then top off with lemon kool-aid or lemonade.

Serving

Mug
****

Lemon Icetini recipe

Description

A delicious recipe for Lemon Icetini, with Bacardi® Limon rum, triple sec, lemonade and Sierra Mist® soda.

Ingredients

1/2 oz Bacardi® Limon rum
1/2 oz triple sec
1 oz lemonade
1 oz Sierra Mist® soda

Instructions

Pour all ingredients into a mixing glass half-filled with ice cubes. Stir well. Strain into a cocktail glass over crushed ice, and serve.

Serving

Cocktail Glass
****

Lemon Joe recipe

Description

A delicious recipe for Lemon Joe, with Bacardi® Limon rum, Absolut® Citron vodka and 7-Up® soda.

Ingredients

1 oz Bacardi® Limon rum
1 oz Absolut® Citron vodka
4 oz 7-Up® soda

Instructions

Pour the Bacardi Limon rum and Absolut Citron vodka into a highball glass filled with ice cubes. Stir well, garnish with a slice of lemon, and serve.

Serving

Highball Glass
****

Lemon Shot recipe

Description

A delicious recipe for Lemon Shot, with Galliano® herbal liqueur, Absolut® Citron vodka, lemon, sugar and Bacardi® 151 rum.

Ingredients

1/2 oz Galliano® herbal liqueur
1/2 oz Absolut® Citron vodka
1 lemon wedge
sugar
Bacardi® 151 rum

Instructions

Mix galliano and absolut citron in a shot glass, lay lemon wedge sprinkled with sugar over glass and pour rum over the wedge and glass. Ignite rum and allow to burn for a moment. Extinguish, shoot quickly, and suck on the lemon.

If it is done correctly, this will taste like a shot of sweet lemonade.

Serving

Shot Glass
****

Lethal Weapon recipe

Description

A delicious recipe for Lethal Weapon, with Bacardi® 151 rum, vodka, Mountain Dew® citrus soda and triple sec.

Ingredients

1 shot Bacardi® 151 rum
2 shots vodka
1 can Mountain Dew® citrus soda
1 dash triple sec

Instructions

Combine all ingredients into a tall glass and serve with ice. As an option, use two cans of mountain dew if the drink seems too strong for you.

Serving

Collins Glass
****

Liberace recipe

Description

A delicious recipe for Liberace, with Kahlua® coffee liqueur, milk and Bacardi® 151 rum.

Ingredients

1/3 shot Kahlua® coffee liqueur
1/3 shot milk
1/3 shot Bacardi® 151 rum

Instructions

Pour in the kahlua, layer the milk on top, and the bacardi 151 on top of the milk. Ignite, let burn for about 10 seconds, blow out and shoot.

Serving

Shot Glass
****

Limon and Ginger recipe

Description

A delicious recipe for Limon and Ginger, with Bacardi® Limon rum and Canada Dry® ginger ale.

Ingredients

1 part Bacardi® Limon rum
1 part Canada Dry® ginger ale

Instructions

Serve pre-chilled or on-the-rocks in a highball glass.

Serving

Highball Glass
****

Limon Delight recipe

Description

A delicious recipe for Limon Delight, with Bacardi® Limon rum and Sunny Delight® orange juice.

Ingredients

1 shot Bacardi® Limon rum
fill with Sunny Delight® orange juice

Instructions

Fill a whiskey sour glass with ice. Add one shot bacardi limon, and fill with sunny delight or orange juice.

Serving

Whiskey Sour Glass
****

Limon Spritzer recipe

Description

A delicious recipe for Limon Spritzer, with Bacardi® Limon rum and Sprite® soda.

Ingredients

2 - 3 oz Bacardi® Limon rum
12 oz chilled can Sprite® soda

Instructions

Pour the Bacardi Limon into a collins glass. Fill with the can of Sprite. Add a piece of lemon, and serve.

Serving

Collins Glass
****

Limon Squeeze recipe

Description

A delicious recipe for Limon Squeeze, with Bacardi® Limon rum and Sprite® soda.

Ingredients

1 1/2 oz Bacardi® Limon rum
12 oz chilled can Sprite® soda

Instructions

Pour the Bacardi Limon into a highball glass. Fill with Sprite or 7-Up. Garnish with a lime, and serve.

Serving

Highball Glass
****

Limona Corona recipe

Description

A delicious recipe for Limona Corona, with Corona® Extra lager and Bacardi® Limon rum.

Ingredients

1 bottle Corona® Extra lager
1 oz Bacardi® Limon rum

Instructions

Open the corona. Fill the empty space in the neck in the bottle with the rum. The bottle should be filled to the top. Plug the bottle with your thumb or the palm of your hand. Turn the bottle upside-down so the rum and beer mix. Turn the bottle rightside-up, unplug, and drink.

****

Limonaide recipe

Description

A delicious recipe for Limonaide, with Bacardi® Limon rum and lemonade.

Ingredients

1 part Bacardi® Limon rum
1 part lemonade

Instructions

Take a tall or short glass and fill with ice. Mix in the bacardi and the lemonade in equal parts.

Serving

Highball Glass
****

Lipstick Cocktail recipe

Description

A delicious recipe for Lipstick Cocktail, with Bacardi® white rum, creme de bananes, cream and grenadine syrup.

Ingredients

2/3 oz Bacardi® white rum
2/3 oz creme de bananes
1 1/3 oz cream
1 1/3 oz grenadine syrup

Instructions

Pour all ingredients into a cocktail shaker half-filled with cracked ice. Shake well, and strain into a small frosted hurricane glass filled with cracked ice. Garnish with a slice of orange and a maraschino cherry, and serve.

Serving

Hurricane Glass
****

Liquid Angel Dust recipe

Description

A delicious recipe for Liquid Angel Dust, with Jim Beam® bourbon whiskey, Tanqueray® gin and Bacardi® dark rum.

Ingredients

1/2 oz Jim Beam® bourbon whiskey
1/2 oz Tanqueray® gin
1/2 oz Bacardi® dark rum

Instructions

Combine all ingredients together in a 1.5-oz shot glass, and serve.

Serving

Shot Glass
****

Liquid Cocaine #3 recipe

Description

A delicious recipe for Liquid Cocaine #3, with Bacardi® 151 rum, Jagermeister® herbal liqueur and Rumple Minze® peppermint liqueur.

Ingredients

1 part Bacardi® 151 rum
1 part Jagermeister® herbal liqueur
1 part Rumple Minze® peppermint liqueur

Instructions

Chill over ice and pour.

Serving

Shot Glass
****

Liquid Cocaine recipe

Description

A delicious recipe for Liquid Cocaine, with Bacardi® 151 rum, Goldschlager® cinnamon schnapps and Jagermeister® herbal liqueur.

Ingredients

1/2 oz Bacardi® 151 rum
1/2 oz Goldschlager® cinnamon schnapps
1/2 oz Jagermeister® herbal liqueur

Instructions

Pour ingredients as listed above into a large shot glass and shoot.

Serving

Shot Glass

****

Liquid Courage recipe

Description

A delicious recipe for Liquid Courage, with milk, ice cream, creme de cacao, vodka and Bacardi® white rum.

Ingredients

1 pint milk
4 - 6 scoops ice cream
8 - 12 oz creme de cacao
6 oz vodka
6 oz Bacardi® white rum

Instructions

Add all ingredients to a blender and liquify until shake-like consistancy. Serve in beer mugs.

Serving

Beer Mug
****

Liquid Ecstasy recipe

Description

A delicious recipe for Liquid Ecstasy, with Bacardi® Limon rum, Midori® melon liqueur, Blue Curacao liqueur, lemon juice and pineapple juice.

Ingredients

30 ml Bacardi® Limon rum
15 ml Midori® melon liqueur
15 ml Blue Curacao liqueur
15 ml lemon juice
90 ml pineapple juice

Instructions

Build bacardi, midori, blue curacao, lemon juice and pineapple juice in that order over ice in a highball glass, or shake and strain into a martini glass. Add a slice of lemon to either the highball glass or the rim of the martini glass. Serve with two straws.

Serving

Highball Glass
****

Liquid Zanex recipe

Description

A delicious recipe for Liquid Zanex, with Jagermeister® herbal liqueur, Goldschlager® cinnamon schnapps, Crown Royal® Canadian whisky and Bacardi® 151 rum.

Ingredients

1/4 oz Jagermeister® herbal liqueur
1/4 oz Goldschlager® cinnamon schnapps
1/4 oz Crown Royal® Canadian whisky
1/4 oz Bacardi® 151 rum

Instructions

Mix ingredients together in a shot glass, and serve.

Serving

Shot Glass
****

Little Bastard recipe

Description

A delicious recipe for Little Bastard, with Bacardi® white rum, orange juice, pineapple juice and 7-Up® soda.

Ingredients

1 oz Bacardi® white rum
1 oz orange juice
1/2 oz pineapple juice
4 oz 7-Up® soda

Instructions

Shake ingredients together with ice in a cocktail shaker. Strain into a highball glass filled with ice cubes, fill with 7-up, and serve.

Serving

Highball Glass
****

Long Walk off a Short Pier recipe

Description

A delicious recipe for Long Walk off a Short Pier, with Bacardi® 151 rum, bourbon whiskey, tequila, vodka, gin, Irish whiskey, Midori® melon liqueur and Coca-Cola®.

Ingredients

1 oz Bacardi® 151 rum
1 oz bourbon whiskey
1 oz tequila
1 oz vodka

1 oz gin
1 oz Irish whiskey
1 oz Midori® melon liqueur
1 1/4 oz Coca-Cola®

Instructions

Pour all ingredients into a tall 16-oz glass filled with ice cubes. Top with Coca-cola, completely or to taste. Stir well, and serve.

Serving

Collins Glass
****

Look Out Below recipe

Description

A delicious recipe for Look Out Below, with Bacardi® 151 rum, lime juice and grenadine syrup.

Ingredients

1 1/2 oz Bacardi® 151 rum
2 tsp fresh lime juice
1 tsp grenadine syrup

Instructions

Pour the Bacardi 151 rum, lime juice and grenadine into a cocktail shaker half-filled with cracked ice. Shake well, strain into an old-fashioned glass 1/2 filled with ice cubes, and serve.

Serving

Old-Fashioned Glass
****

Love Byte recipe

Description

A delicious recipe for Love Byte, with Bacardi® gold rum, triple sec, Amaretto Di Saronno® liqueur, Malibu® pineapple rum, pineapple juice and grenadine syrup.

Ingredients

1 oz Bacardi® gold rum
1/2 oz triple sec
1/2 oz Amaretto Di Saronno® liqueur
1 oz Malibu® pineapple rum
3 oz pineapple juice
1 oz grenadine syrup

Instructions

Pour all ingredients into a cocktail shaker filled with ice cubes. Shake well. Pour all contents into a highball glass. Garnish with a piece of pineapple and a maraschino cherry, and serve.

Serving

Highball Glass
****

Luftschlange recipe

Description

A delicious recipe for Luftschlange, with Bacardi® white rum, Malibu® coconut rum, creme de cacao, almond syrup, coconut cream and pineapple juice.

Ingredients

2 cl Bacardi® white rum
2 cl Malibu® coconut rum
1 shot creme de cacao
1 shot almond syrup
1 1/2 cl coconut cream
6 cl pineapple juice

Instructions

Shake all ingredients. Strain into a highball glass, and serve.

Serving

Highball Glass
****

Lunar Landing recipe

Description

A delicious recipe for Lunar Landing, with Bacardi® Limon rum and Zima.

Ingredients

2 oz Bacardi® Limon rum
6 oz Zima

Instructions

Stir ingredients together well in a collins glass filled with ice cubes, and serve.

Serving

Collins Glass
****

MacArthur Cocktail recipe

Description

A delicious recipe for MacArthur Cocktail, with Bacardi® dark rum, Jamaican dark rum, triple sec and egg.

Ingredients

1 1/2 oz Bacardi® dark rum
3 dashes Jamaican dark rum
3/4 oz triple sec
1 dash egg white

Instructions

Shake the rums, triple sec and egg white together in a cocktail shaker half-filled with ice. Strain into a cocktail glass, and serve.

Serving

Cocktail Glass
****

Martha Stewart recipe

Description

A delicious recipe for Martha Stewart, with Bacardi® 151 rum, Wild Turkey® 101 bourbon whiskey and grenadine syrup.

Ingredients

1/2 oz Bacardi® 151 rum
1/2 oz Wild Turkey® 101 bourbon whiskey
1 tsp grenadine syrup

Instructions

Pour the Bacardi 151 rum and Wild Turkey 101 bourbon whiskey into a shot glass. Stir, and float grenadine on top. Shoot immediately.

Serving

Shot Glass
****

Mary Elizabeth Wagoner recipe

Description

A delicious recipe for Mary Elizabeth Wagoner, with vodka, Bacardi® 151 rum, Everclear® alcohol, sweet and sour mix and lime juice.

Ingredients

1 oz vodka
1/2 oz Bacardi® 151 rum
1/2 oz Everclear® alcohol

1 oz sweet and sour mix
1/2 oz lime juice

Instructions

Shake the vodka, rum, everclear and sour mix in a cocktail shaker half-filled with ice cubes. Strain into a cocktail glass, add lime juice on top and serve.

Serving

Cocktail Glass
****

Mayan Sacrafice recipe

Description

A delicious recipe for Mayan Sacrafice, with tequila, Bacardi® 151 rum, Kahlua® coffee liqueur and vodka.

Ingredients

1/2 oz tequila
1/2 oz Bacardi® 151 rum
1 oz Kahlua® coffee liqueur
1 oz vodka

Instructions

Pour Kahlua into a small rocks or old-fashioned glass. Add Bacardi 151 and tequila, and top with vodka. Ignite the top on fire, and allow to burn for a few seconds. Extinguish, quickly take the straw to the bottom of the glass and consume.

Serving

Old-Fashioned Glass
****

Miami Vice recipe

Description

A delicious recipe for Miami Vice, with Bacardi® 151 rum, pina colada mix and daiquiri mix.

Ingredients

5 oz Bacardi® 151 rum
1 package frozen pina colada mix
1 package frozen daiquiri mix

Instructions

1. Mix pina colada with 2.5 oz. of rum w/ ice. Set aside.

2. Mix daiquiri with 2.5 oz. of rum w/ ice.

3. While frozen, add pina colada mix to a cocktail glass. Add the daiquiri mix on top, keeping it seperated from the pina colada mix. Serve.

Serving

Cocktail Glass
****

Midori Illusion recipe

Description

A delicious recipe for Midori Illusion, with Midori® melon liqueur, vodka, Bacardi® white rum, Cointreau® orange liqueur, Blue Curacao liqueur, pineapple juice and lemonade.

Ingredients

1 oz Midori® melon liqueur
1 oz vodka
1 oz Bacardi® white rum
1 oz Cointreau® orange liqueur
1/2 oz Blue Curacao liqueur
pineapple juice
lemonade

Instructions

Pour the Midori melon liqueur, vodka, Bacardi white rum, Cointeau, blue curacao and pineapple juice (to taste) into a highball glass filled with ice cubes. Stir well. Top with lemonade, stir again gently, and serve.

Serving

Highball Glass
****

Midori Mai Tai recipe

Description

A delicious recipe for Midori Mai Tai, with Midori® melon liqueur, Bacardi® Limon rum, triple sec, pineapple juice and sweet and sour mix.

Ingredients

1 oz Midori® melon liqueur
1 oz Bacardi® Limon rum
1/2 oz triple sec
2 oz pineapple juice
1 oz sweet and sour mix

Instructions

Pour all ingredients into a cocktail shaker half-filled with ice cubes. Shake well, strain into a highball glass almost filled with ice cubes, and serve.

Serving

Highball Glass
****

Mind Bomb recipe

Description

A delicious recipe for Mind Bomb, with Everclear® alcohol, Bacardi® 151 rum, strawberry schnapps and grenadine syrup.

Ingredients

1 1/2 oz Everclear® alcohol
1 1/2 oz Bacardi® 151 rum
1 1/2 oz strawberry schnapps
1 tbsp grenadine syrup

Instructions

Pour all ingredients into a highball glass half-filled with ice cubes, stir and serve.

Serving

Highball Glass
****

Mind Eraser #4 recipe

Description

A delicious recipe for Mind Eraser #4, with vodka, Midori® melon liqueur, Bacardi® 151 rum and lime juice.

Ingredients

1/2 oz vodka
1/2 oz Midori® melon liqueur
1/2 oz Bacardi® 151 rum
1/2 oz lime juice

Instructions

Shake with ice, strain into a shot glass and serve.

Serving

Shot Glass
****

Mogul Masher recipe

Description

A delicious recipe for Mogul Masher, with cocoa powder, Bacardi® 151 rum, Rumple Minze® peppermint liqueur, water and whipped cream.

Ingredients

1 package cocoa powder
1 oz Bacardi® 151 rum
1 oz Rumple Minze® peppermint liqueur
8 oz hot water
1 1/2 oz whipped cream

Instructions

Mix hot chocolate as per usual (in a 12 oz. glass or larger) and add liquors. Top with whipped cream.

Serving

Highball Glass
****

Mojito Tampa recipe

Description

A delicious recipe for Mojito Tampa, with Bacardi® silver rum, soda water, sugar, ice, mint and lime.

Ingredients

2 oz Bacardi® silver rum
2 oz soda water
1 tbsp sugar
3/4 cup ice
4 sprigs of large mint leaves
4 fresh lime slices

Instructions

Squeeze and add the lime slices into an old-fashioned glass. Add the mint leaves and decorate with mint leaves on the stem. Add the ice, sugar and soda water to make simple syrup. Use a large wooden spoon to crush and infuse the ingredients together. Add the rum last, and serve.

Serving

Old-Fashioned Glass
****

Mongolian Dingbat recipe

Description

A delicious recipe for Mongolian Dingbat, with Bacardi® white rum, Tia Maria® coffee liqueur and ice cream.

Ingredients

1 oz Bacardi® white rum
1 oz Tia Maria® coffee liqueur
1 scoop ice cream

Instructions

Combine the Bacardi white rum, Tia Maria coffee liqueur and ice cream in a blender. Blend well. Pour into a cocktail glass, and serve.

Serving

Cocktail Glass
****

Moose Juice #2 recipe

Description

A delicious recipe for Moose Juice #2, with beer, orange juice, vodka, triple sec, cranberry juice, cherry juice and Bacardi® O rum.

Ingredients

12 oz beer
6 oz orange juice
2 oz vodka
2 oz triple sec
1 1/2 oz cranberry juice
1 oz cherry juice
1 oz Bacardi® O rum

Instructions

Stir ingredients together in a jug or pitcher, and serve.

Serving

Jug
****

Mr. Gerbik recipe

Description

A delicious recipe for Mr. Gerbik, with Bombay Sapphire® gin, Dr. Pepper® soda and Bacardi® 151 rum.

Ingredients

2 oz Bombay Sapphire® gin
6 - 8 oz Dr. Pepper® soda
1/4 oz Bacardi® 151 rum

Instructions

Stir the gin together with the Dr. Pepper in a highball glass. Carefully layer the Bacardi 151 rum on top, ignite and serve.

Serving

Highball Glass

****

Muddy Puddle recipe

Description

A delicious recipe for Muddy Puddle, with vodka, Bacardi® gold rum, Coca-Cola®, lemonade, blackcurrant juice and orange juice.

Ingredients

70 cl bottle vodka
70 cl bottle Bacardi® gold rum
2 liters bottle Coca-Cola®
2 liters bottle lemonade
1 liter carton blackcurrant juice
1 liter carton orange juice

Instructions

Pour all ingredients into a large punch bowl with plenty of ice. Stir vigorously, and serve into cups.

Serving

Punch Bowl
****

Mustang Ranch Freebie recipe

Description

A delicious recipe for Mustang Ranch Freebie, with Bacardi® white rum, sweet and sour mix, grenadine syrup and grapefruit juice.

Ingredients

3/4 oz Bacardi® white rum
1/2 oz sweet and sour mix
1/4 oz grenadine syrup
1 oz grapefruit juice

Instructions

Pour all ingredients into a champagne flute filled with shaven ice, and serve.

Serving

Champagne Flute
****

Naked Twister Shots recipe

Description

A delicious recipe for Naked Twister Shots, with Bacardi® Limon rum and Pepsi® Twist cola.

Ingredients

1 shot Bacardi® Limon rum
1 shot Pepsi® Twist cola

Instructions

Pour both ingredients into seperate shot glasses. Drink half the Pepsi, shoot the Bacardi Limon, then finish the Pepsi shot. Rinse and repeat.

Serving

Shot Glass
****

Napalm Bomb recipe

Description

A delicious recipe for Napalm Bomb, with Jagermeister® herbal liqueur, Bacardi® 151 rum and orange juice.

Ingredients

2/3 oz Jagermeister® herbal liqueur
1/3 oz Bacardi® 151 rum
1 oz orange juice

Instructions

Stir ingredients together in a double-shot glass, and shoot.

Serving

Shot Glass
****

Naval Destroyer recipe

Description

A delicious recipe for Naval Destroyer, with limeade, Bacardi® white rum and MGD® Lite lager.

Ingredients

1 can frozen limeade concentrate
1 can Bacardi® white rum
3 cans MGD® Lite lager

Instructions

Thaw limeade concentrate and put in pitcher. Pour Bacardi rum into the empty limeade can until full, then transfer to pitcher. Add 3 beers to pitcher, and serve over ice in glasses.

Serving

Pitcher
****

Navy Grog recipe

Description

A delicious recipe for Navy Grog, with Bacardi® light rum, Bacardi® gold rum, Bacardi® dark rum, Grand Marnier® orange liqueur, grapefruit juice, orange juice and pineapple juice.

Ingredients

1/2 oz Bacardi® light rum
1/2 oz Bacardi® gold rum
1/2 oz Bacardi® dark rum
1/2 oz Grand Marnier® orange liqueur
1 oz grapefruit juice
1 oz orange juice
1 oz pineapple juice

Instructions

Pour liquors into an ice-filled collins glass. Add juices, shake, and garnish with an orange wedge and pineapple chunk.

Serving

Collins Glass
****

No Pressure recipe

Description

A delicious recipe for No Pressure, with strawberry daiquiri mix, pina colada mix, Curacao orange liqueur and Bacardi® 151 rum.

Ingredients

1 part frozen strawberry daiquiri mix
1 part pina colada mix
1 splash Curacao orange liqueur
1 shot Bacardi® 151 rum

Instructions

Fill a hurricane glass one-third full with frozen strawberry daiquiri mix. Carefully layer the frozen pina colada mix until two-thirds full. Add a splash of blue curacao on top, and insert a straw. Fill with 151 proof rum.

Serving

Hurricane Glass
****

Norling Special recipe

Description

A delicious recipe for Norling Special, with Bacardi® Limon rum, Midori® melon liqueur, 7-Up® soda and cranberry juice.

Ingredients

3 cl Bacardi® Limon rum
3 cl Midori® melon liqueur
7-Up® soda
cranberry juice

Instructions

Pour midori and bacardi limon into a highball glass half-filled with crushed ice. Fill with equal parts 7-up and cranberry juice.

Serving

Highball Glass
****

Novicain recipe

Description

A delicious recipe for Novicain, with Bacardi® 151 rum, DeKuyper® Razzmatazz liqueur and sweet and sour mix.

Ingredients

1 oz Bacardi® 151 rum
1 oz DeKuyper® Razzmatazz liqueur
1 oz sweet and sour mix

Instructions

Combine all ingredients together in a cocktail shaker with a few ice cubes. Shake well, strain into a shot glass, and serve.

Serving

Shot Glass
****

Nuclear Rainbow recipe

Description

A delicious recipe for Nuclear Rainbow, with grenadine syrup, Rumple Minze® peppermint liqueur, Jagermeister® herbal liqueur, Midori® melon liqueur, Crown Royal® Canadian whisky, Bacardi® 151 rum and amaretto almond

Ingredients

1/2 oz grenadine syrup
1/2 oz Rumple Minze® peppermint liqueur

1/2 oz Jagermeister® herbal liqueur
1/2 oz Midori® melon liqueur
1/2 oz Crown Royal® Canadian whisky
1/2 oz Bacardi® 151 rum
1/2 oz amaretto almond liqueur

Instructions

Carefully layer, in order, into a glass.

Serving

Champagne Flute
****

Nuclear Slush recipe

Description

A delicious recipe for Nuclear Slush, with Absolut® Citron vodka, Bacardi® Limon rum, Midori® melon liqueur, Blue Curacao liqueur and sweet and sour mix.

Ingredients

3/4 oz Absolut® Citron vodka
3/4 oz Bacardi® Limon rum
1/2 oz Midori® melon liqueur
1/2 oz Blue Curacao liqueur
sweet and sour mix

Instructions

Fill a blender about 3/4 with crushed ice and add liqueurs. Mix and add the sour mix until the mixture funnels in the blender. The final result should be thick. Add more ice if necessary. Pour into a hurricane glass, and serve.

Serving

Hurricane Glass
****

Nuthugger recipe

Description

A delicious recipe for Nuthugger, with Bacardi® 151 rum, vodka, lime juice and beer.

Ingredients

1 oz Bacardi® 151 rum
1 oz vodka
3 oz lime juice
beer

Instructions

Pour in liquors, add lime juice, and fill with beer. Serve unstirred.

****

O & Cranberry recipe

Description

A delicious recipe for O & Cranberry, with Bacardi® orange rum, cranberry juice and orange.

Ingredients

1 1/2 oz Bacardi® orange rum
5 oz cranberry juice
1 orange wedge

Instructions

Stir together in a tall glass over ice. Garnish with an orange wedge.

Serving

Collins Glass
****

O & Cream recipe

Description

A delicious recipe for O & Cream, with Bacardi® orange rum and Irish cream.

Ingredients

1 1/2 oz Bacardi® orange rum
1 1/2 oz Irish cream

Instructions

Shake ingredients with ice and serve in a rocks glass over ice.

Serving

Old-Fashioned Glass
****

O & Tonic recipe

Description

A delicious recipe for O & Tonic, with Bacardi® orange rum, tonic water and orange.

Ingredients

1 1/2 oz Bacardi® orange rum
6 oz tonic water
1 twist orange peel

Instructions

Serve in a tall glass with ice.

Serving

Collins Glass
****

O Circle Martini recipe

Description

A delicious recipe for O Circle Martini, with Bacardi® orange rum, Amaretto Di Saronno® liqueur and cream.

Ingredients

1 1/2 oz Bacardi® orange rum
1/2 oz Amaretto Di Saronno® liqueur
1 splash cream

Instructions

Shake ingredients with ice, strain and serve into a chilled martini glass. Garnish with a twist of orange.

Serving

Cocktail Glass
****

O Cosmopolitan recipe

Description

A delicious recipe for O Cosmopolitan, with Bacardi® orange rum, triple sec, lime juice, cranberry juice and orange.

Ingredients

2 oz Bacardi® orange rum
1 oz triple sec
1/2 oz lime juice
1 splash cranberry juice
1 orange wedge

Instructions

Serve on the rocks. Garnish with a wedge of orange.

Serving

Champagne Saucer

****

O Look Martini Cocktail recipe

Description

A delicious recipe for O Look Martini Cocktail, with Bacardi® orange rum, grapefruit juice, triple sec, sweet and sour mix and lemon-lime soda.

Ingredients

2 oz Bacardi® orange rum
1/2 oz pink grapefruit juice
1/2 oz triple sec
1/2 oz sweet and sour mix
1 splash lemon-lime soda

Instructions

Serve together in a sugar-rimmed glass garnished with a slice of grapefruit.

Serving

Cocktail Glass
****

O Madras recipe

Description

A delicious recipe for O Madras, with Bacardi® orange rum, cranberry juice, orange juice, maraschino cherry and orange.

Ingredients

1 1/2 oz Bacardi® orange rum
4 oz cranberry juice
1 oz orange juice
1 maraschino cherry
1 slice orange

Instructions

Blend ingredients with ice and serve in a tall glass. Garnish with a maraschino cherry and a slice of orange.

Serving

Collins Glass
****

O Martini Cocktail recipe

Description

A delicious recipe for O Martini Cocktail, with Bacardi® orange rum, Martini & Rossi® extra dry vermouth and orange.

Ingredients

2 oz Bacardi® orange rum
1/4 oz Martini & Rossi® extra dry vermouth
1 twist orange peel

Instructions

Serve in a rocks glass over ice, or straight up in a martini glass.

Serving

Cocktail Glass
****

O My Martini recipe

Description

A delicious recipe for O My Martini, with Bacardi® orange rum, Blue Curacao liqueur, sweet and sour mix and grenadine syrup.

Ingredients

2 oz Bacardi® orange rum
1 oz Blue Curacao liqueur
1 splash sweet and sour mix
top with grenadine syrup

Instructions

Shake ingredients with ice. Strain into a chilled martini glass. Top with grenadine.

Serving

Cocktail Glass
****

O Thing recipe

Description

A delicious recipe for O Thing, with Amp® energy drink and Bacardi® O rum.

Ingredients

12 oz can Amp® energy drink
2 - 4 oz Bacardi® O rum

Instructions

Pour the can of Amp energy drink into a tall glass. Add the Bacardi O rum (more or less acccording to taste), and serve.

Serving

Collins Glass
****

Old-Fashioned Rum and Coke recipe

Description

A delicious recipe for Old-Fashioned Rum and Coke, with Bacardi® white rum and Coca-Cola®.

Ingredients

4 oz Bacardi® white rum
8 oz Coca-Cola®

Instructions

Serve in an old-fashioned glass.

Serving

Old-Fashioned Glass

****

Ooh La La Martini Cocktail recipe

Description

A delicious recipe for Ooh La La Martini Cocktail, with Bacardi® orange rum, orange juice and triple sec.

Ingredients

1 oz Bacardi® orange rum
1 oz orange juice
1 splash triple sec

Instructions

Shake ingredients with ice, strain and serve in a chilled martini glass. Garnish with a slice of orange.

Serving

Cocktail Glass
****

Oompa Loompa recipe

Description

A delicious recipe for Oompa Loompa, with Bacardi® Razz rum and Stoli® Razberi vodka.

Ingredients

1/2 oz Bacardi® Razz rum
1/2 oz Stoli® Razberi vodka

Instructions

Pour Bacardi Razz raspberry-flavored rum and Stoli Razberi raspberry-flavored vodka into a shot glass, in equal parts, and serve.

Serving

Shot Glass

****

Orang-A-Tang recipe

Description

A delicious recipe for Orang-A-Tang, with vodka, Bacardi® 151 rum, triple sec, orange juice, sweet and sour mix and grenadine syrup.

Ingredients

1 oz vodka
1 oz Bacardi® 151 rum
1/2 oz triple sec
6 oz orange juice
1 splash sweet and sour mix
1 splash grenadine syrup

Instructions

Pour the vodka, triple sec, orange juice, sour mix and grenadine into a cocktail shaker half-filled with ice cubes. Shake well, and strain into a large brandy snifter half-filled with ice. Float the Bacardi 151 on top, garnish with tropical fruit, and serve.

Serving

Brandy Snifter
****

Orange Hawaiian recipe

Description

A delicious recipe for Orange Hawaiian, with Bacardi® orange rum and Hawaiian punch.

Ingredients

100 ml Bacardi® orange rum
3 liters bottle Hawaiian punch

Instructions

Pour the Bacardi O orange-flavored rum into a blender. Add ice, enough so that it will be slushy when you drink it. Pour in as much Hawaiian punch as you can, and blend. Pour into a pitcher, make a glass for yourself, and store the rest in the fridge.

Serving

Pitcher
****

Orange Jeff recipe

Description

A delicious recipe for Orange Jeff, with Captain Morgan® Parrot Bay coconut rum, Bacardi® white rum, Bacardi® dark rum, orange juice and banana.

Ingredients

1 oz Captain Morgan® Parrot Bay coconut rum
1 oz Bacardi® white rum
1 oz Bacardi® dark rum
8 oz orange juice
1 banana

Instructions

Combine all ingredients in a blender. Blend until smooth, pour into a hurricane glass. Garnish with slices or pieces of tropical fruit, add a straw, and serve.

Serving

Hurricane Glass
****

Orange Rush recipe

Description

A delicious recipe for Orange Rush, with Bacardi® orange rum, peach schnapps, orange juice, pineapple juice and cranberry juice.

Ingredients

1 oz Bacardi® orange rum
1/2 oz peach schnapps
2 oz orange juice

1 oz pineapple juice
1 oz cranberry juice

Instructions

Blend ingredients with ice. Serve in a tall glass and garnish with a slice of orange.

Serving

Collins Glass
****

Orange Soda recipe

Description

A delicious recipe for Orange Soda, with Bacardi® orange rum, cranberry juice and soda.

Ingredients

1 oz Bacardi® orange rum
2 oz cranberry juice
3 oz soda

Instructions

Pour Bacardi O over ice in a highball glass. Add cranberry juice, and top off with soda. Garnish with a slice of lime on the glass, and serve.

Serving

Highball Glass
****

Orangesicle recipe

Description

A delicious recipe for Orangesicle, with Bacardi® orange rum, cream and orange juice.

Ingredients

1 1/2 oz Bacardi® orange rum
1 1/2 oz cream
1/2 oz orange juice

Instructions

Blend ingredients and serve in a powdered sugar rimmed glass. Garnish with an orange wheel.

Serving

Cocktail Glass
****

Original Zombie recipe

Description

A delicious recipe for Original Zombie, with Bacardi® light rum, Bacardi® dark rum, creme de almond, triple sec, sweet and sour mix, orange juice and Bacardi® 151 rum.

Ingredients

1 oz Bacardi® light rum
1 oz Bacardi® dark rum
1/2 oz creme de almond
1/2 oz triple sec
sweet and sour mix
orange juice
1/2 oz Bacardi® 151 rum

Instructions

Pour light rum, dark rum, creme de almond and triple sec into an ice-filled hurricane glass. Almost-fill with equal parts of sweet and sour and orange juice. Top with 151 rum. Add a large straw, and serve unstirred.

Serving

Hurricane Glass
****

Orthoniatis recipe

Description

A delicious recipe for Orthoniatis, with kiwi liqueur, Bacardi® white rum and pineapple juice.

Ingredients

2 oz kiwi liqueur
1 oz Bacardi® white rum
4 oz pineapple juice

Instructions

Pour the kiwi liqueur, Bacardi white rum and pineapple juice into a cocktail shaker with 5 ice cubes. Shake well, pour into a collins glass, and serve.

Serving

Collins Glass
****

Otter Pop #2 recipe

Description

A delicious recipe for Otter Pop #2, with Bacardi® Limon rum, Malibu® coconut rum, Stoli® Vanil vodka, Midori® melon liqueur, Blue Curacao liqueur, sweet and sour mix, 7-Up® soda and grenadine syrup. Also lists simi

Ingredients

1 oz Bacardi® Limon rum
1 oz Malibu® coconut rum
1 oz Stoli® Vanil vodka
1/2 oz Midori® melon liqueur
1/2 oz Blue Curacao liqueur
2 dashes sweet and sour mix
7-Up® soda
2 - 3 drops grenadine syrup

Instructions

Add liquors and sweet and sour mix to a cocktail shaker. Fill with 7-up or sprite, and top with grenadine. Shake, and strain into a pint glass over ice.

Serving

Beer Mug
****

Otter Pop recipe

Description

A delicious recipc for Otter Pop, with Bacardi® white rum, Blue Curacao liqueur, sweet and sour mix and 7-Up® soda.

Ingredients

1/2 oz Bacardi® white rum
1/2 oz Blue Curacao liqueur
1/4 oz sweet and sour mix
1/4 oz 7-Up® soda

Instructions

Combine all ingredients in an ice-filled shaker, and strain into a shot glass.

Serving

Shot Glass
****

Pain Killer recipe

Description

A delicious recipe for Pain Killer, with Midori® melon liqueur, cranberry juice, orange juice, pineapple juice and Bacardi® 151 rum.

Ingredients

1 1/2 oz Midori® melon liqueur
cranberry juice

orange juice
pineapple juice
1/2 oz Bacardi® 151 rum

Instructions

Pour midori melon liqueur in an ice-filled collins glass. Almost-fill, with equal parts; cranberry, orange, and pineapple juice. Add rum, garnish with a cherry, and serve.

Serving

Collins Glass
****

Painkiller recipe

Description

A delicious recipe for Painkiller, with White Mozart® chocolate liqueur, Bacardi® black rum, coconut syrup and orange liqueur.

Ingredients

2 oz White Mozart® chocolate liqueur
1 oz Bacardi® black rum
1 dash coconut syrup
1 dash orange liqueur

Instructions

Mix well in a shaker with three or four ice cubes. Strain into an old-fashioned glass, garnish with a pineapple piece, and serve.

Serving

Old-Fashioned Glass
****

Parappa the Drunk Rappa recipe

Description

A delicious recipe for Parappa the Drunk Rappa, with Bacardi® 151 rum, amaretto almond liqueur, Southern Comfort® peach liqueur and cherry cola.

Ingredients

1 shot Bacardi® 151 rum
1 shot amaretto almond liqueur
1 shot Southern Comfort® peach liqueur
1 can cherry cola

Instructions

Pour shots over ice, add coke and strain into a collins   glass.

Serving

Collins Glass
****

Party Boy recipe

Description

A delicious recipe for Party Boy, with pink lemonade, Bacardi® 151 rum, triple sec, Absolut® Citron vodka, sweet and sour mix, sugar and lemon.

Ingredients

1 1/2 oz pink lemonade
1 oz Bacardi® 151 rum
1/2 oz triple sec
1/2 oz Absolut® Citron vodka
1 dash sweet and sour mix
1 tsp sugar
1 slice lemon

Instructions

Rub a lemon slice on the edge of a whiskey sour glass. Dip the edge of the glass in sugar. Add pink lemonade and a dash of sour mix. Then add Bacardi, triple sec and Absolut Citron. Stir. Lick around the edge of the glass then take the shot.

Serving

Whiskey Sour Glass
****

Passion Beach recipe

Description

A delicious recipe for Passion Beach, with Passoa® liqueur, DeKuyper® Peachtree schnapps, Bacardi® Limon rum, grapefruit juice and orange juice.

Ingredients

3 cl Passoa® liqueur
2 cl DeKuyper® Peachtree schnapps
2 cl Bacardi® Limon rum
8 cl grapefruit juice
2 cl orange juice

Instructions

Shake all ingredients with ice, strain into an ice-filled highball glass, and serve with fresh fruit on the rim of the glass.

Serving

Highball Glass
****

Pearl Diver recipe

Description

A delicious recipe for Pearl Diver, with Bacardi® white rum, triple sec, Midori® melon liqueur and sweet and sour mix.

Ingredients

1/2 oz Bacardi® white rum
1/2 oz triple sec
1/2 oz Midori® melon liqueur
sweet and sour mix

Instructions

Mix all ingredients together, shake, and strain over ice in a highball glass.

Serving

Highball Glass
****

Pedro Collins recipe

Description

A delicious recipe for Pedro Collins, with Bacardi® Limon rum, sweet and sour mix, 7-Up® soda and club soda.

Ingredients

1 1/2 oz Bacardi® Limon rum
1 splash sweet and sour mix
2 oz 7-Up® soda
2 oz club soda

Instructions

Pour bacardi limon into an ice-filled collins glass. Add sweet and sour mix, and fill with equal parts of club soda and 7-up.

Serving

Collins Glass
****

Pensacola Bushwacker recipe

Description

A delicious recipe for Pensacola Bushwacker, with cream of coconut, Kahlua® coffee liqueur, Bacardi® black rum, creme de cacao, half-and-half and vanilla ice   cream.

Ingredients

4 oz cream of coconut
2 oz Kahlua® coffee liqueur
1 oz Bacardi® black rum
1 oz creme de cacao
4 oz half-and-half
vanilla ice cream

Instructions

Pour all ingredients into a blender (ice cream optional) with two cups of ice, and blend until mixed. Serve in a hurricane glass.

Serving

Hurricane Glass
****

Penthouse recipe

Description

A delicious recipe for Penthouse, with tequila, Bacardi® Limon rum and lime juice.

Ingredients

2 1/2 cl tequila
2 1/2 cl Bacardi® Limon rum
4 dashes lime juice

Instructions

Pour ingredients into a shot glass, and shoot. Chase with a lime wedge.

Serving

Shot Glass
****

Perfect Kiss recipe

Description

A delicious recipe for Perfect Kiss, with Bacardi® white rum, DeKuyper® Peachtree schnapps, Sprite® soda and strawberries.

Ingredients

2 cl Bacardi® white rum
2 cl DeKuyper® Peachtree schnapps
Sprite® soda
strawberries

Instructions

Pour white rum and peachtree schnapps over crushed ice in a margarita glass. Top with sprite, and gently place one half-strawberry underneath the layer of crushed ice. Serve.

Serving

Margarita Glass
****

Petite Fleur recipe

Description

A delicious recipe for Petite Fleur, with grapefruit juice, Bacardi® white rum and Cointreau® orange liqueur.

Ingredients

1 part grapefruit juice
2 parts Bacardi® white rum
1 part Cointreau® orange liqueur

Instructions

Shake and strain into a cocktail glass.

Serving

Cocktail Glass
****

Pick Me Up Jose recipe

Description

A delicious recipe for Pick Me Up Jose, with Bacardi® 151 rum and Jose Cuervo® Especial gold tequila.

Ingredients

1/2 oz Bacardi® 151 rum
1/2 oz Jose Cuervo® Especial gold tequila

Instructions

Lay a shot glass in a clean ash tray right side up, and start to pour the drinks into the glass until they overflow into the ash tray. Ignite the liquor, blow it out, take the shot from the shot glass, then drink out of the ash tray.

Serving

Shot Glass
****

Pineapple Fuck-Me-Up recipe

Description

A delicious recipe for Pineapple Fuck-Me-Up, with Bacardi® 151 rum, pineapple juice and triple sec.

Ingredients

2 oz Bacardi® 151 rum
3/4 oz pineapple juice
1 splash triple sec

Instructions

Pour Bacardi 151 into a cocktail glass. Add pineapple juice, a splash of triple sec, and serve.

Serving

Cocktail Glass
****

Pineappleless Pineapple Juice recipe

Description

A delicious recipe for Pineappleless Pineapple Juice, with Southern Comfort® peach liqueur, Bacardi® 151 rum, 7-Up® soda, orange juice and Coca-Cola®.

Ingredients

4 1/2 oz Southern Comfort® peach liqueur
1 splash Bacardi® 151 rum
3 oz 7-Up® soda
4 oz orange juice
4 oz Coca-Cola®

Instructions

Pour southern comfort to the first line of a 16 oz. solo brand plastic cup. Add bacardi 151 rum, 7-up, orange juice, and coca-cola. Swirl briefly around in the cup and serve.

Serving

Cup
****

Pink Cement recipe

Description

A delicious recipe for Pink Cement, with Bacardi® Razz rum and Tequila Rose® strawberry cream liqueur.

Ingredients

1/2 oz Bacardi® Razz rum
1/2 oz Tequila Rose® strawberry cream liqueur

Instructions

Pour both ingredients into a shot glass, and serve.

Serving

Shot Glass
****

Pink Clyt recipe

Description

A delicious recipe for Pink Clyt, with Bacardi® white rum, Absolut® vodka, Tanqueray® gin, triple sec, cranberry juice and pineapple juice.

Ingredients

1/2 oz Bacardi® white rum
1/2 oz Absolut® vodka
1/2 oz Tanqueray® gin
1/4 oz triple sec
1 splash cranberry juice
1 splash pineapple juice

Instructions

Shake in a cocktail shaker with ice cubes. Pour into an old-fashioned glass, garnish with a cherry, and serve.

Serving

Old-Fashioned Glass
****

Pink Limon recipe

Description

A delicious recipe for Pink Limon, with Bacardi® Limon rum, sweet and sour mix and cranberry juice.

Ingredients

1 1/2 oz Bacardi® Limon rum
2 oz sweet and sour mix
1/2 oz cranberry juice

Instructions

Shake and strain into a chilled, sugar-rimmed cocktail glass. Garnish with a lemon wheel.

Serving

Cocktail Glass
****

Pipeline recipe

Description

A delicious recipe for Pipeline, with Bacardi® white rum, powdered sugar, apricot brandy and lemon juice.

Ingredients

1 1/2 oz Bacardi® white rum
1/2 tsp powdered sugar
1/4 oz apricot brandy
3/4 oz lemon juice

Instructions

Shake well over ice cubes in a shaker. Strain into a chilled cocktail glass, and serve.

Serving

Cocktail Glass
****

Pit Bull On Crack recipe

Description

A delicious recipe for Pit Bull On Crack, with Jose Cuervo® Especial gold tequila, Jagermeister® herbal liqueur, Jim Beam® bourbon whiskey and Bacardi® 151 rum.

Ingredients

1 part Jose Cuervo® Especial gold tequila
1 part Jagermeister® herbal liqueur
1 part Jim Beam® bourbon whiskey
1 part Bacardi® 151 rum

Instructions

Combine ingredients, all pre-chilled, in a shot glass. Serve.

Serving

Shot Glass
****

Portland Coffee recipe

Description

A delicious recipe for Portland Coffee, with Bacardi® 151 rum, Kahlua® coffee liqueur, triple sec, cinnamon, nutmeg, sugar, whipped cream and coffee.

Ingredients

1 shot Bacardi® 151 rum
1 shot Kahlua® coffee liqueur
2 splashes triple sec
3 dashes cinnamon
3 dashes nutmeg
1/4 cup sugar
1 squirt whipped cream

1/2 cup coffee

Instructions

Dip the rim of an irish coffee cup into a puddle of triple sec, then a plate of sugar. Pour in the rum, kahlua, and one splash of triple sec. Light with a match to crystalize the sugar-rim. Add cinnamon and nutmeg, and pour in the coffee (and extinguish flame) until three-quarters full. Top with whipped cream, and serve.

Serving

Irish Coffee Cup
****

Postman recipe

Description

A delicious recipe for Postman, with Absolut® vodka, Bacardi® 151 rum, orange juice, cranberry juice and grenadine syrup.

Ingredients

2 oz Absolut® vodka
1 oz Bacardi® 151 rum
2 oz orange juice
1 oz cranberry juice
1 splash grenadine syrup

Instructions

Chill, shake, and pour over ice cubes in a shot glass.

Serving

Shot Glass
****

Psycho recipe

Description

A delicious recipe for Psycho, with Bacardi® white rum, Galliano® herbal liqueur, orange juice, pineapple juice and grenadine syrup.

Ingredients

4 cl Bacardi® white rum
2 cl Galliano® herbal liqueur
8 cl orange juice
8 cl pineapple juice
2 cl grenadine syrup

Instructions

Shake all ingredients with ice, and strain into a cocktail glass. Garnish with an orange slice, pineapple chunk and maraschino cherry.

Serving
Cocktail Glass
****

Puerto Rican Popper recipe

Description
A delicious recipe for Puerto Rican Popper, with Bacardi® Limon rum, Passoa® liqueur, cranberry juice and Champagne.

Ingredients
1 oz Bacardi® Limon rum
1 oz Passoa® liqueur
3 oz cranberry juice
1 splash Champagne

Instructions
Pour the Bacardi Limon and Passoa into a highball glass filled with ice cubes. Top with cranberry juice, and stir well. Splash with champagne, and serve.

Serving
Highball Glass
****

Punch In The Pants recipe

Description
A delicious recipe for Punch In The Pants, with Bacardi® orange rum, Bacardi® Limon rum, triple sec, sweet and sour mix and orange soda.

Ingredients
1 oz Bacardi® orange rum
1 oz Bacardi® Limon rum
1 splash triple sec
1 splash sweet and sour mix
3 oz orange soda

Instructions
Blend ingredients with ice and serve.

Serving
Highball Glass
****

Ramcooler recipe

Description

A delicious recipe for Ramcooler, with Bacardi® white rum, Galliano® herbal liqueur and lime juice.

Ingredients

1 1/4 oz Bacardi® white rum
1/2 oz Galliano® herbal liqueur
2 oz lime juice

Instructions

Pour all ingredients into a 10 oz old-fashioned glass, fill with crushed ice and shake. Garnish with a red cherry and a slice of lime.

Serving

Old-Fashioned Glass
****

Ramshanked recipe

Description

A delicious recipe for Ramshanked, with Bacardi Breezer®, Malibu® coconut rum, Southern Comfort® peach liqueur and lemon.

Ingredients

1 bottle Bacardi Breezer®
2 oz Malibu® coconut rum
2 oz Southern Comfort® peach liqueur
1 slice lemon

Instructions

Place the lemon slice at the bottom of a highball glass. Add ice, and pour the rum and southern comfort. Finally, add the bottle of Bacardi. Stir and serve.

Serving

Highball Glass
****

Real Romulan Ale recipe

Description

A delicious recipe for Real Romulan Ale, with Bacardi® 151 rum, Everclear® alcohol and Blue Curacao liqueur.

Ingredients

375 ml Bacardi® 151 rum
375 ml Everclear® alcohol

375 ml Blue Curacao liqueur

Instructions

Combine ingredients in a (just over) one-liter bottle. Chill in freezer for two hours. Serve in shot glasses.

Serving

Shot Glass
****

Red Dwarf recipe

Description

A delicious recipe for Red Dwarf, with Bacardi® white rum, lemon juice, orange juice, peach schnapps and creme de cassis.

Ingredients

2 oz Bacardi® white rum
1/3 oz lemon juice
2 oz orange juice
1 oz peach schnapps
1/3 oz creme de cassis

Instructions

Mix rum, lemon juice, orange juice and peach schnapps together with plenty of ice in a shaker. Pour into a chilled highball glass. Add creme de cassis; allowing it to form a layer at the bottom of the glass. Garnish with cherries, orange or lemon to taste, and serve.

Serving

Highball Glass
****

Red Eisentrout recipe

Description

A delicious recipe for Red Eisentrout, with Absolut® vodka, Bombay Sapphire® gin, Bacardi® white rum, Grand Marnier® orange liqueur, Surge® citrus soda and cherry juice.

Ingredients

1/2 oz Absolut® vodka
1/2 oz Bombay Sapphire® gin
1/2 oz Bacardi® white rum
1/2 oz Grand Marnier® orange liqueur
Surge® citrus soda
cherry juice

Instructions

Pour liquors over ice in a collins glass, and almost fill with surge soda. Top off with cherry juice, and shake. Garnish with a cherry, and serve.

Serving

Collins Glass
****

Red Headed Stepchild #2 recipe

Description

A delicious recipe for Red Headed Stepchild #2, with Bacardi® light rum and Mountain Dew® Code Red soda.

Ingredients

1 1/2 oz Bacardi® light rum
6 1/2 oz Mountain Dew® Code Red soda

Instructions

Pour Bacardi into a collins glass filled with ice. Add Code red mountain dew, and serve.

Serving

Collins Glass
****

Red Hurricane recipe

Description

A delicious recipe for Red Hurricane, with Bacardi® Limon rum, tequila and cranberry juice.

Ingredients

1 oz Bacardi® Limon rum
1 oz tequila
3 oz cranberry juice

Instructions

Pour over ice in a highball glass. Stir, and serve.

Serving

Highball Glass
****

Red Ox recipe

Description

A delicious recipe for Red Ox, with Bacardi® light rum, Malibu® coconut rum, pineapple juice, cranberry juice, sweet and sour mix and grenadine syrup.

Ingredients

1 oz Bacardi® light rum
1/2 oz Malibu® coconut rum
1 oz pineapple juice
1/2 oz cranberry juice
sweet and sour mix
grenadine syrup

Instructions

Pour rums and juices into a pint glass one-quarter filled with ice. Almost fill with sweet and sour, top with grenadine, and mix.

Serving

Beer Mug
****

Red Rooster recipe

Description

A delicious recipe for Red Rooster, with Bacardi® 151 rum, creme de noyaux, guava juice and grenadine syrup.

Ingredients

1 1/4 oz Bacardi® 151 rum
1/2 oz creme de noyaux
6 oz guava juice
1 splash grenadine syrup

Instructions

Build drink in a collins glass.

Serving

Collins Glass
****

Rocket Fuel #3 recipe

Description

A delicious recipe for Rocket Fuel #3, with Bacardi® 151 rum, vodka and Blue Curacao liqueur.

Ingredients

1/2 shot Bacardi® 151 rum
1/4 shot vodka
1/4 shot Blue Curacao liqueur

Instructions

Pour ingredients, in order, into a shot glass. Serve.

Serving

Shot Glass
****

Rootbeer Piss recipe

Description

A delicious recipe for Rootbeer Piss, with Mug® root beer, Bacardi® 151 rum and Aftershock® Hot & Cool cinnamon schnapps.

Ingredients

8 oz can Mug® root beer
1 1/2 oz Bacardi® 151 rum
1/2 oz Aftershock® Hot & Cool cinnamon schnapps

Instructions

Fill an iced beer mug halfway with ice cubes. Add Bacardi 151, then Aftershock, followed by an entire can of Mug root beer (or until mug is full). Stir briskly with a spoon and serve.

Serving

Beer Mug
****

Rum Aid recipe

Description

A delicious recipe for Rum Aid, with Bacardi® 151 rum, Malibu® coconut rum, Captain Morgan® Original spiced rum, Grand Marnier® orange liqueur, sweet and sour mix and ginger ale.

Ingredients

1 oz Bacardi® 151 rum
1 oz Malibu® coconut rum
1 oz Captain Morgan® Original spiced rum
2 tbsp Grand Marnier® orange liqueur
1 ml sweet and sour mix
1 part ginger ale

Instructions

Shake and strain over ice in a margarita glass. Add a twist of lemon, and serve.

Serving

Margarita Glass
****

Rumage recipe

Description

A delicious recipe for Rumage, with Bacardi® Superior rum, Captain Morgan® Original spiced rum, Malibu® coconut rum, orange juice and pineapple juice.

Ingredients

1 oz Bacardi® Superior rum
1 oz Captain Morgan® Original spiced rum
2 oz Malibu® coconut rum
4 oz orange juice
4 oz pineapple juice

Instructions

Pour Bacardi Superior rum and Captain Morgan spiced rum into a collins glass. Add Malibu coconut rum, and juices. Stir and serve.

Serving

Highball Glass
****

Rummple recipe

Description

A delicious recipe for Rummple, with orange juice, light rum, coconut rum and Bacardi® Limon rum.

Ingredients

3 oz orange juice
1/2 oz light rum
1/2 oz coconut rum
1/2 oz Bacardi® Limon rum

Instructions

Mix all ingredients with ice, pour into a highball glass, and serve.

Serving

Highball Glass
****

Sacrilicious recipe

Description

A delicious recipe for Sacrilicious, with Bacardi® Limon rum, Midori® melon liqueur and lime juice.

Ingredients

1/3 oz Bacardi® Limon rum
1/3 oz Midori® melon liqueur
1/3 oz lime juice

Instructions

Chill and strain into a shot glass.

Serving

Shot Glass

****

Sake O Martini recipe

Description

A delicious recipe for Sake O Martini, with Bacardi® orange rum, sake rice wine and cranberry juice.

Ingredients

2 oz Bacardi® orange rum
1/4 oz sake rice wine
1/4 oz cranberry juice

Instructions

Shake with ice and strain into a chilled martini glass.

Serving

Cocktail Glass

****

San Juan Cooler recipe

Description

A delicious recipe for San Juan Cooler, with Bacardi® white rum, dry vermouth and pineapple juice.

Ingredients

2 oz Bacardi® white rum
3/4 oz dry vermouth
fill with pineapple juice

Instructions

Fill a highball glass with ice.

Add rum and dry vermouth. Fill with pineapple juice and serve.

Serving

Highball Glass

****

San Juan Tea recipe

Description

A delicious recipe for San Juan Tea, with Bacardi® Limon rum, Bacardi® 151 rum, sweet and sour mix and Coca-Cola®.

Ingredients

1 1/2 oz Bacardi® Limon rum
1/2 oz Bacardi® 151 rum
3 oz sweet and sour mix
fill with Coca-Cola®

Instructions

Shake liquor and sour mix. Garnish with lemon wedge.

Serving

Collins Glass
****

Satin Rouge recipe

Description

A delicious recipe for Satin Rouge, with Bacardi® orange rum, Bacardi® Tropico rum, cherry juice, pineapple juice and lemon.

Ingredients

1 1/4 oz Bacardi® orange rum
1/2 oz Bacardi® Tropico rum
1/4 oz cherry juice
1/2 oz pineapple juice
1 twist lemon peel

Instructions

Serve in a chilled cocktail glass. Garnish with a twist of lemon.

Serving

Cocktail Glass
****

Screaming Dead Nazi recipe

Description

A delicious recipe for Screaming Dead Nazi, with Jagermeister® herbal liqueur, Bacardi® 151 rum and Rumple Minze® peppermint liqueur.

Ingredients

1 part Jagermeister® herbal liqueur
1 part Bacardi® 151 rum
1 part Rumple Minze® peppermint liqueur

Instructions

Pour all in shot glass, one by one. Set a flame, blow it out, and enjoy.

Serving

Shot Glass
****

Shetty Classic recipe

Description

A delicious recipe for Shetty Classic, with Ricard® pastis, Bacardi® white rum and Absolut® vodka.

Ingredients

1 oz Ricard® pastis
1 oz Bacardi® white rum
1 oz Absolut® vodka

Instructions

Pour Ricard, Bacardi rum and Absolut vodka into a bowl filled with sugar. Set on fire (use extreme caution) and let the sugar dissolve. Allow the drink to cool, and serve in a cocktail glass.

Serving

Cocktail Glass
****

Shut the Hell Up recipe

Description

A delicious recipe for Shut the Hell Up, with Bacardi® 151 rum, Crown Royal® Canadian whisky, Jagermeister® herbal liqueur, Everclear® alcohol and grenadine syrup.

Ingredients

1/2 part Bacardi® 151 rum
1 part Crown Royal® Canadian whisky
1 part Jagermeister® herbal liqueur
1/2 part Everclear® alcohol
2 splashes grenadine syrup

Instructions

Pour Jager at bottom of glass. Mix Crown, Everclear, & 151 separately to layer on top of the Jager. Splash the Grenadine. Attempt to shoot & shut the hell up.

Serving

Old-Fashioned Glass
****

Sky Blue Fallout recipe

Description

A delicious recipe for Sky Blue Fallout, with Blue Curacao liqueur, gin, vodka, triple sec, tequila, Bacardi® 151 rum, sweet and sour mix, 7-Up® soda and ice.

Ingredients

2 counts Blue Curacao liqueur
2 counts gin
2 counts vodka
2 counts triple sec
2 counts tequila
2 counts Bacardi® 151 rum
1 part sweet and sour mix
1 part 7-Up® soda
1 part ice

Instructions

Mix all ingredients except 7-Up in a mixing glass. Pour into a hurricane glass and add the 7-Up. Stir lightly with a straw and serve.

Serving

Hurricane Glass
****

Skylab Fallout recipe

Description

A delicious recipe for Skylab Fallout, with Absolut® vodka, Bacardi® 151 rum, gold tequila, gin, Everclear® alcohol, Blue Curacao liqueur and pineapple juice.

Ingredients

1/2 oz Absolut® vodka
1/2 oz Bacardi® 151 rum
1/2 oz gold tequila
1/2 oz gin
1/2 oz Everclear® alcohol
1/2 oz Blue Curacao liqueur
1/2 oz pineapple juice

Instructions

Put plenty of ice in glass pour rum and everclear first refill with ice - put your tequila, gin, vodka and your blue curacao in. Put your pinapple juice in and shake serve with a lemon slice and cherry.

Serving

Hurricane Glass

****

Skylab recipe

Description

A delicious recipe for Skylab, with vodka, Bacardi® light rum, peach schnapps, Blue Curacao liqueur, pineapple juice, orange juice and Sprite® soda.

Ingredients

1 oz vodka
1 oz Bacardi® light rum
1/2 oz peach schnapps
1/2 oz Blue Curacao liqueur
1 splash pineapple juice
1 splash orange juice
1 splash Sprite® soda

Instructions

Pour all ingredients into a shaker and strain into a chilled glass.

Serving

Hurricane Glass
****

Slushy recipe

Description

A delicious recipe for Slushy, with Bacardi® white rum, Blue Curacao liqueur, DeKuyper® Razzmatazz liqueur and pineapple juice.

Ingredients

2 oz Bacardi® white rum
1 1/2 oz Blue Curacao liqueur
1 oz DeKuyper® Razzmatazz liqueur
4 oz pineapple juice

Instructions

Mix drink with crushed ice or blend with 2 1/2 scoops of ice. For added enjoyment stick a straw in the middle and drink for a slushy rush.

Serving

Margarita Glass
****

Smooth Operator recipe

Description

A delicious recipe for Smooth Operator, with Bacardi® Limon rum, Malibu® coconut rum, peach schnapps, triple sec, 7-Up® soda, ice and fruit.

Ingredients

2 oz Bacardi® Limon rum
1 oz Malibu® coconut rum
2 oz peach schnapps
2 oz triple sec
1 can 7-Up® soda
ice
fruit

Instructions

Combine all ingredients, except 7-Up, in blender. Divide into 2 jars. Top with 7-Up, stir well.

****

Snowballs recipe

Description

A delicious recipe for Snowballs, with vodka, Bacardi® light rum, peach schnapps and ice.

Ingredients

3 oz vodka
2 oz Bacardi® light rum
1 oz peach schnapps
1 - 2 cups ice

Instructions

Pour all ingredients into a blender. Blend on high until the ice is crushed completely. Pour into a collins glass, and serve into two highball glasses or one very tall glass.

Serving

Highball Glass
****

Sobo recipe

Description

A delicious recipe for Sobo, with Sobe® Energy drink and Bacardi® orange rum.

Ingredients

10 1/2 oz chilled Sobe® Energy drink
4 1/2 oz Bacardi® orange rum

Instructions

Pour Sobe Energy into a collins glass. Add Bacardi O, and serve.

Serving

Collins Glass
****

Soft Serbian recipe

Description

A delicious recipe for Soft Serbian, with Smirnoff® vodka, Pernod® licorice liqueur, Bacardi® 151 rum, orange juice, tonic water and crushed ice.

Ingredients

2 cl Smirnoff® vodka
1 cl Pernod® licorice liqueur
1 cl Bacardi® 151 rum
12 cl orange juice
12 cl tonic water
crushed ice

Instructions

Mix alcohol, then juice and tonic water. Add crushed ice and drink.

Serving

Highball Glass
****

Sophisticate recipe

Description

A delicious recipe for Sophisticate, with Bacardi® orange rum, melon liqueur, lemon-lime soda and cranberry juice.

Ingredients

1 oz Bacardi® orange rum
1/2 oz melon liqueur
1/2 oz lemon-lime soda
1/2 oz cranberry juice

Instructions

Serve over ice in a cocktail glass. Garnish with melon, strawberry and sugar-coated orange.

Serving

Cocktail Glass
****

Sour Kiss recipe

Description

A delicious recipe for Sour Kiss, with Bacardi® Limon rum, DeKuyper® Cheri-Beri Pucker schnapps, DeKuyper® Grape Pucker schnapps, sugar syrup, sweet and sour mix and club soda.

Ingredients

1/2 oz Bacardi® Limon rum
1/2 oz DeKuyper® Cheri-Beri Pucker schnapps
1/2 oz DeKuyper® Grape Pucker schnapps
1/4 oz sugar syrup
1/2 oz sweet and sour mix
1 splash club soda

Instructions

Combine all ingredients into a mixing tin. Stir over ice and strain into a cocktail glass. Cocktail glass should be sugar rimmed and garnished with a lemon.

Serving

Cocktail Glass
****

Southern Bacardi recipe

Description

A delicious recipe for Southern Bacardi, with Bacardi® 151 rum, Southern Comfort® peach liqueur and Coca-Cola®.

Ingredients

4 oz Bacardi® 151 rum
4 oz Southern Comfort® peach liqueur
4 oz Coca-Cola®

Instructions

Pour ingredients over a few ice cubes in a hurricane glass, stir and serve.

Serving

Hurricane Glass
****

Space Odyssey recipe

Description

A delicious recipe for Space Odyssey, with Bacardi® 151 rum, Malibu® coconut rum, pineapple juice, orange juice and grenadine syrup.

Ingredients

1 shot Bacardi® 151 rum
1 shot Malibu® coconut rum
1 shot pineapple juice
orange juice
1 dash grenadine syrup

Instructions

Fill glass with ice and add shots of bacardi and malibu. Add splash of pineapple juice and top with orange juice. Add grenadine for color and garnish with cherries.

Serving

Cocktail Glass
****

Sparkplug recipe

Description

A delicious recipe for Sparkplug, with Bacardi® 151 rum and Rumple Minze® peppermint liqueur.

Ingredients

1/2 shot Bacardi® 151 rum
1/2 shot Rumple Minze® peppermint liqueur

Instructions

Pour Bacardi 151 in the shot glass first, then pour Rumplminze on top, do not mix.

Serving

Shot Glass
****

Squirting Orgasm recipe

Description

A delicious recipe for Squirting Orgasm, with Jose Cuervo® Especial gold tequila, Everclear® alcohol, Jagermeister® herbal liqueur and Bacardi® 151 rum.

Ingredients

1/4 oz Jose Cuervo® Especial gold tequila
1/4 oz Everclear® alcohol
1/4 oz Jagermeister® herbal liqueur
1/4 oz Bacardi® 151 rum

Instructions

Pour all ingredients, in equal parts, into a shot glass. Stir and serve.

Serving

Shot Glass
****

Start Me Up recipe

Description

A delicious recipe for Start Me Up, with Absolut® vodka, tequila, Absolut® Kurant vodka and Bacardi® dark rum.

Ingredients

3 cl Absolut® vodka
1 cl tequila
1 cl Absolut® Kurant vodka
1 cl Bacardi® dark rum

Instructions

Mix everything in a container (bottle, glass etc.), then it is ready for consumption.

Serving

Shot Glass
****

Strawberry Dream recipe

Description

A delicious recipe for Strawberry Dream, with strawberries, strawberry schnapps, Bacardi® dark rum, cream, pineapple juice, ice cubes and vanilla ice cream.

Ingredients

3 strawberries
3/4 oz strawberry schnapps
3/4 oz Bacardi® dark rum
3/4 oz cream
3/4 oz pineapple juice
4 ice cubes
2 scoops vanilla ice cream

Instructions

Add all ingredients to a blender. Blend for 1 minute or until drink is smooth. Pour into glass and serve immediately.

Serving

Hurricane Glass
****

Strawberry Kiss recipe

Description

A delicious recipe for Strawberry Kiss, with orange juice, strawberry schnapps, Bacardi® light rum, cranberry juice and brandy.

Ingredients

2 oz orange juice
3/4 oz strawberry schnapps
3/4 oz Bacardi® light rum
1/2 oz cranberry juice
1/4 oz brandy

Instructions

Add all ingredients in the order shown above, and stir well. Add ice cubes and serve.

Serving

Hurricane Glass
****

Strawberry-Peach Daiquiri recipe

Description

A delicious recipe for Strawberry-Peach Daiquiri, with strawberries, Bacardi® white rum, DeKuyper® Peachtree schnapps, sugar and lemon juice.

Ingredients

2 cups sliced strawberries
3 oz Bacardi® white rum
1 oz DeKuyper® Peachtree schnapps
1/4 cup sugar
1 squeeze lemon juice

Instructions

Add strawberries, Bacardi white rum, DeKuyper Peachtree schnapps, sugar, and lemon juice to a blender with one cup of crushed ice (more or less if desired). Blend until icy with no chunks of ice remaining. Pour into a hurricane glass, garnish with a slice or two of strawberry, and serve.

Serving

Hurricane Glass
****

Suicidal recipe

Description

A delicious recipe for Suicidal, with vodka, Everclear® alcohol and Bacardi® 151 rum.

Ingredients

1/3 oz vodka
1/3 oz Everclear® alcohol
1/3 oz Bacardi® 151 rum

Instructions

Pour ingredients in equal parts into a shot glass, and serve.

Serving

Shot Glass
****

Sunset Breeze recipe

Description

A delicious recipe for Sunset Breeze, with Absolut® vodka, Absolut® Citron vodka, Bacardi® Tropico rum, lime juice, cherry heering and simple syrup.

Ingredients

1/2 oz Absolut® vodka
1/2 oz Absolut® Citron vodka
1 1/2 oz Bacardi® Tropico rum
1/2 oz fresh lime juice
1/2 oz cherry heering
1/2 oz simple syrup

Instructions

Shake all ingredients with ice and strain into a cocktail glass. Garnish with a twist of orange peel, and serve.

Serving

Cocktail Glass
****

Sunset Martini Cocktail recipe

Description

A delicious recipe for Sunset Martini Cocktail, with Bacardi® orange rum and lemonade.

Ingredients

1 1/2 oz Bacardi® orange rum
3 oz lemonade

Instructions

Shake with ice and strain into a sugar-rimmed martini glass.

Serving

Cocktail Glass
****

Super O Martini Cocktail recipe

Description

A delicious recipe for Super O Martini Cocktail, with Bacardi® orange rum, Bacardi® Tropico rum, Amaretto Di Saronno® liqueur and triple sec.

Ingredients

2 oz Bacardi® orange rum
1 oz Bacardi® Tropico rum
1/4 oz Amaretto Di Saronno® liqueur
1/4 oz triple sec

Instructions

Shake and serve in a chillled glass with an orange garnish.

Serving

Cocktail Glass
****

Super Slice recipe

Description

A delicious recipe for Super Slice, with Bacardi® orange rum and Pepsi® Orange Slice soda.

Ingredients

4 oz Bacardi® orange rum
8 oz Pepsi® Orange Slice soda

Instructions

Pour Bacardi O into a highball glass. Fill with Orange Slice, and serve.

Serving

Highball Glass
****

Sweaty Mexican recipe

Description

A delicious recipe for Sweaty Mexican, with Bacardi® 151 rum, tequila and Tabasco® sauce.

Ingredients

2 oz Bacardi® 151 rum
2 oz tequila
2 oz Tabasco® sauce

Instructions

Pour all ingredients into an old-fashioned glass, stir, and shoot.

Serving

Old-Fashioned Glass
****

Sweaty Shooter recipe

Description

A delicious recipe for Sweaty Shooter, with Bacardi® 151 rum and Tabasco® sauce.

Ingredients

1/2 oz Bacardi® 151 rum
1 splash Tabasco® sauce

Instructions

Pour rum into a shot glass. Top with tabasco sauce, and serve.

Serving

Shot Glass
****

Tahitian Treat recipe

Description

A delicious recipe for Tahitian Treat, with Bacardi® Limon rum, amaretto almond liqueur, cranberry juice, Sprite® soda and ice cubes.

Ingredients

1 oz Bacardi® Limon rum
1 oz amaretto almond liqueur
4 oz cranberry juice
fill with Sprite® soda
ice cubes

Instructions

Fill highball glass with ice. Add liquor, juice, and then sprite.

Serving

Highball Glass

****

Tango Martini Cocktail recipe

Description

A delicious recipe for Tango Martini Cocktail, with Bacardi® orange rum, raspberry liqueur, triple sec, pineapple juice, cranberry juice and orange.

Ingredients

2 oz Bacardi® orange rum
1/2 oz raspberry liqueur
1/2 oz triple sec
1 oz pineapple juice
1 splash cranberry juice
1 orange

Instructions

Shake ingredients with ice and strain into a chilled martini glass. Squeeze orange juice into the bottom of the glass, and garnish with a twist of orange.

Serving

Cocktail Glass
****

Terminator recipe

Description

A delicious recipe for Terminator, with Bacardi® 151 rum and Rumple Minze® peppermint liqueur.

Ingredients

1/2 oz Bacardi® 151 rum
1/2 oz Rumple Minze® peppermint liqueur

Instructions

151 first, then Rumple Minze.

Serving

Shot Glass
****

Texas Pink Cloud recipe

Description

A delicious recipe for Texas Pink Cloud, with Bacardi® white rum, Absolut® vodka, Jose Cuervo® Especial gold tequila, grenadine syrup, pina colada mix, sweet and sour mix, margarita mix and ice.

Ingredients

3 oz Bacardi® white rum
2 oz Absolut® vodka
1 oz Jose Cuervo® Especial gold tequila
1/2 oz grenadine syrup
3 oz pina colada mix
2 oz sweet and sour mix
1 oz margarita mix
3 - 4 cups ice

Instructions

Pour all ingredients into a blender, add 3 - 4 cups of ice and blend until all ice is chopped fine. Should be the consistentency of a daiquiri or colada. Pour into a pitcher ready to serve.

Serving

Pitcher
****

Texas Sling recipe

Description

A delicious recipe for Texas Sling, with Kahlua® coffee liqueur, Irish cream, amaretto almond liqueur, Bacardi® 151 rum and cream.

Ingredients

1/2 oz Kahlua® coffee liqueur
1/2 oz Irish cream
1/2 oz amaretto almond liqueur
1/2 oz Bacardi® 151 rum
11 oz cream

Instructions

Blend with ice until smooth. Serve in a tulip glass, topped with whipped cream.

Serving

Hurricane Glass
****

Texas Sunset recipe

Description

A delicious recipe for Texas Sunset, with white rum, apricot brandy, Bacardi® 151 rum, orange juice, lemon juice, sugar syrup, egg and grenadine syrup.

Ingredients

3/4 oz white rum

1/2 oz apricot brandy
1/2 oz Bacardi® 151 rum
2 oz orange juice
1 oz lemon juice
1/2 oz sugar syrup
1 tsp egg white
3/4 oz grenadine syrup

Instructions

Shake all ingredients (except grenadine) briefly with three-quarters of a glassful of broken ice. Pour unstrained into a collins glass, sprinkle grenadine on top, and serve unstirred.

Serving

Collins Glass
****

The Cherry Bomb recipe

Description

A delicious recipe for The Cherry Bomb, with cherry, Absolut® vodka, cinnamon schnapps and Bacardi® light rum.

Ingredients

1 cherry
2 tsp Absolut® vodka
1 tsp cinnamon schnapps
1 tsp Bacardi® light rum

Instructions

Put the cherry into the shot glass. Add the Cinnamon Schnapps (be careful it is real strong). Then add the Rum and top of with the Vodka. More Vodka can be used. Slam it.

Serving

Shot Glass
****

The Dark Side recipe

Description

A delicious recipe for The Dark Side, with amaretto almond liqueur, Bacardi® 151 rum, dark creme de cacao, Kahlua® coffee liqueur, triple sec, vanilla ice cream and chocolate syrup.

Ingredients

3/4 oz amaretto almond liqueur
3/4 oz Bacardi® 151 rum
3/4 oz dark creme de cacao

3/4 oz Kahlua® coffee liqueur
3/4 oz triple sec
3 scoops vanilla ice cream
chocolate syrup

Instructions

Mix all ingredients in mixer, pour into highball glass.

Optional - Frost glass with chocolate syrup before pouring.

Serving

Highball Glass
****

The End Of The World recipe

Description

A delicious recipe for The End Of The World, with Bacardi® 151 rum, Wild Turkey® bourbon whiskey and vodka.

Ingredients

1/2 oz Bacardi® 151 rum
1/2 oz Wild Turkey® bourbon whiskey
1/2 oz vodka

Instructions

Serve warm. Straight into the shot glass.

Serving

Shot Glass
****

The Hague recipe

Description

A delicious recipe for The Hague, with Southern Comfort® peach liqueur, Crown Royal® Canadian whisky, peach schnapps, Bacardi® 151 rum, cranberry juice, pineapple juice and orange juice.

Ingredients

1/2 oz Southern Comfort® peach liqueur
1/2 oz Crown Royal® Canadian whisky
1/2 oz peach schnapps
1/2 oz Bacardi® 151 rum
2 oz cranberry juice
2 oz pineapple juice
2 oz orange juice

Instructions

Pour all ingredients into a cocktail shaker. Shake, strain into an old-fashioned glass, and serve.

Serving

Old-Fashioned Glass
****

The Hurtado recipe

Description

A delicious recipe for The Hurtado, with Rumple Minze® peppermint liqueur, sambuca, Bacardi® white rum, cranberry juice and oranges.

Ingredients

2 oz Rumple Minze® peppermint liqueur
2 oz sambuca
1/2 oz Bacardi® white rum
2 oz cranberry juice
3 oz oranges

Instructions

Mix all ingredients in a glass with a lot of ice, shake well and serve.

Serving

Hurricane Glass
****

The Leap Frog recipe

Description

A delicious recipe for The Leap Frog, with Bacardi® orange rum, triple sec, sweet and sour mix, orange juice and maraschino cherries.

Ingredients

1 oz Bacardi® orange rum
1 oz triple sec
1 1/2 oz sweet and sour mix
1/2 oz fresh orange juice
2 maraschino cherries

Instructions

Shake ingredients and strain into a cocktail glass. Garnish with a lime and two maraschino cherries on both ends of the lime.

Serving

Cocktail Glass

****

The Marvin recipe

Description

A delicious recipe for The Marvin, with vodka, rum, gin, tequila, Captain Morgan® Parrot Bay coconut rum, Bacardi® Limon rum, Chambord® raspberry liqueur and sweet and sour mix.

Ingredients

1/2 oz vodka
1/2 oz rum
1/2 oz gin
1/2 oz tequila
1/2 oz Captain Morgan® Parrot Bay coconut rum
1/2 oz Bacardi® Limon rum
1 oz Chambord® raspberry liqueur
1 oz sweet and sour mix

Instructions

Add all liquors and sour mix to a large cocktail glass filled with ice, stir and serve.

Serving

Cocktail Glass
****

The Other Half recipe

Description

A delicious recipe for The Other Half, with triple sec, amaretto almond liqueur and Bacardi® 151 rum.

Ingredients

3/4 oz triple sec
3/4 oz amaretto almond liqueur
Bacardi® 151 rum

Instructions

Carefully layer the triple sec, amaretto, and rum into a shot glass. Turn off the lights, ignite the rum (use caution) to warm rim of glass, and carefully blow out the flame. Serve immediately.

Serving

Shot Glass
****

The Perfect Ten recipe

Description

A delicious recipe for The Perfect Ten, with Bacardi® Limon rum, Pisang Ambon® liqueur, lemon juice and Sprite® soda.

Ingredients

4 cl Bacardi® Limon rum
2 cl Pisang Ambon® liqueur
lemon juice
Sprite® soda

Instructions

Pour the liquors into an old-fashioned glass. Fill with equal parts of lemon juice and sprite.

Serving

Old-Fashioned Glass
****

The Quickening recipe

Description

A delicious recipe for The Quickening, with Goldschlager® cinnamon schnapps, vodka and Bacardi® 151 rum.

Ingredients

2 1/2 oz Goldschlager® cinnamon schnapps
2 1/2 oz vodka
2 1/2 oz Bacardi® 151 rum

Instructions

Pour all ingredients over ice in a sugar-frosted-rimmed or cinnamon-frosted-rimmed collins glass, and serve.

Serving

Collins Glass
****

The Shanaynay recipe

Description

A delicious recipe for The Shanaynay, with Bacardi® 151 rum, water and lemonade mix.

Ingredients

2 oz Bacardi® 151 rum
12 oz water
powdered lemonade mix

Instructions

Mix the water and rum, and add powdered lemonade mix to taste. Stir, and serve.

Serving

Collins Glass
****

The Shearer Special recipe

Description

A delicious recipe for The Shearer Special, with Bacardi® Limon rum and cranberry juice.

Ingredients

1 fifth Bacardi® Limon rum
cranberry juice

Instructions

Mix fifth of a gallon of bacardi to a splash of cranberry juice.

Serving

Punch Bowl
****

The Whammie recipe

Description

A delicious recipe for The Whammie, with Bacardi® light rum, Captain Morgan® Original spiced rum, Bacardi® 151 rum, peach brandy, creme de cassis, creme de bananes, raspberry liqueur, orange juice, pineapple juice and grenadine syr

Ingredients

1 oz Bacardi® light rum
1 oz Captain Morgan® Original spiced rum
1 oz Bacardi® 151 rum
1 oz peach brandy
1 oz creme de cassis
1 oz creme de bananes
1 oz raspberry liqueur
orange juice
pineapple juice
grenadine syrup

Instructions

Fill a 20 ounce glass with ice. Add the 7 shots. Finish off with with equal parts orange and pineapple juice. Add grenadine until it turns pink. Top with cherries.

Serving

Hurricane Glass
****

Third Rail recipe

Description

A delicious recipe for Third Rail, with Bacardi® anejo rum, Orange Curacao liqueur and limes.

Ingredients

1 1/2 oz Bacardi® anejo rum
3/4 oz Orange Curacao liqueur
juice of 1/2 limes

Instructions

Shake and strain into a chilled, sugar-rimmed cocktail glass. Garnish with a lime twist.

Serving

Cocktail Glass
****

Thorazine recipe

Description

A delicious recipe for Thorazine, with Jagermeister® herbal liqueur, Rumple Minze® peppermint liqueur and Bacardi® 151 rum.

Ingredients

1/2 oz Jagermeister® herbal liqueur
1/2 oz Rumple Minze® peppermint liqueur
1/2 oz Bacardi® 151 rum

Instructions

Add all three ingredients in order to a shot glass. Best served with top layer on fire. (For effect only)

Serving

Shot Glass
****

Thunder And Lighting recipe

Description

A delicious recipe for Thunder And Lighting, with Rumple Minze® peppermint liqueur and Bacardi® 151 rum.

Ingredients

1/2 oz Rumple Minze® peppermint liqueur
1/2 oz Bacardi® 151 rum

Instructions

Mix in shaker and serve.

Tidal Wave recipe

Description

A delicious recipe for Tidal Wave, with Tanqueray® gin, light rum, Smirnoff® vodka, peach schnapps, orange juice, pineapple juice, grenadine syrup and Bacardi® 151 rum.

Ingredients

1/2 oz Tanqueray® gin
1/2 oz light rum
1/2 oz Smirnoff® vodka
1/2 oz peach schnapps
2 oz orange juice
2 oz pineapple juice
1 dash grenadine syrup
Bacardi® 151 rum

Instructions

Pour gin, vodka, rum and peach schnapps over ice in a collins glass. Add orange and pineapple juices, a dash of grenadine, and float 151 rum on top. Garnish with a piece of fresh cut pineapple. The wave will sweep you away!

Serving

Collins Glass
****

Trinidad recipe

Description

A delicious recipe for Trinidad, with Bacardi® white rum, Angostura® bitters and Coca-Cola®.

Ingredients

1 1/2 oz Bacardi® white rum
4 dashes Angostura® bitters
5 oz Coca-Cola®

Instructions

Build in a highball glass over ice, garnish with a wedge of lime, and serve.

Serving

Highball Glass
****

Tropical Suicide recipe

Description

A delicious recipe for Tropical Suicide, with Bacardi® Superior rum, Malibu® coconut rum, Jose Cuervo® Especial gold tequila, pineapple juice, cranberry juice and orange juice.

Ingredients

1 oz Bacardi® Superior rum
2 oz Malibu® coconut rum
1/2 oz Jose Cuervo® Especial gold tequila
4 oz pineapple juice
4 oz cranberry juice
4 oz orange juice

Instructions

Pour Bacardi rum into a collins glass. Add Malibu rum, Jose Cuervo tequila, pineapple juice, cranberry juice and orange juice. Stir, add a few ice cubes, and serve.

Serving

Collins Glass
****

Tsunami #2 recipe

Description

A delicious recipe for Tsunami #2, with Blue Curacao liqueur, Bacardi® white rum, Mountain Dew® citrus soda and kiwi.

Ingredients

1 1/2 oz Blue Curacao liqueur
1/2 oz Bacardi® white rum
Mountain Dew® citrus soda
1 slice kiwi

Instructions

Place kiwi slice in the bottom of the glass. Add alcohols. Fill with mountain dew.

Serving

Cocktail Glass
****

Utar recipe

Description

A delicious recipe for Utar, with light rum, dark rum, lemonade, Bacardi® 151 rum and Captain Morgan® Original spiced rum.

Ingredients

1 part light rum
1 part dark rum
1 part lemonade
1 part Bacardi® 151 rum
1 part Captain Morgan® Original spiced rum

Instructions

Mix in glass and serve.

Serving

Collins Glass
****

Vampire Juice recipe

Description

A delicious recipe for Vampire Juice, with CocoRibe® coconut rum, Blue Curacao liqueur, Bacardi® Limon rum and orange juice.

Ingredients

1 oz CocoRibe® coconut rum
1 oz Blue Curacao liqueur
1 oz Bacardi® Limon rum
8 oz orange juice

Instructions

Pour coconut rum, curacao and bacardi into a shaker with three or four ice cubes. Strain into a collins glass, fill with orange juice, and serve.

Serving

Collins Glass
****

Vanilla Vargas recipe

Description

A delicious recipe for Vanilla Vargas, with Bacardi® 151 rum, Crown Royal® Canadian whisky, vanilla liqueur and Pepsi® cola.

Ingredients

1 shot Bacardi® 151 rum
1 shot Crown Royal® Canadian whisky
4 shots vanilla liqueur
1 can Pepsi® cola

Instructions

Pour liquors, in order, into a highball glass half-filled with crushed ice. Top with pepsi, stir well with a barspoon, and serve.

Serving

Highball Glass
****

Voodoo Dew recipe

Description

A delicious recipe for Voodoo Dew, with Bacardi® 151 rum and Mountain Dew® citrus soda.

Ingredients

3 shots Bacardi® 151 rum
1 can Mountain Dew® citrus soda

Instructions

Pour shots into a mason jar or large glass. Add mountain dew, mix well, and serve.

Serving

Mason Jar
****

Wave Runner recipe

Description

A delicious recipe for Wave Runner, with Bacardi® light rum, cranberry juice and Sprite® soda.

Ingredients

2 parts Bacardi® light rum
2 parts cranberry juice
fill with Sprite® soda

Instructions

Pour rum and cranberry juice into a tall glass. Slowly add sprite, stopping immediately when the color changes from red to pink.

Serving

Collins Glass
****

Weakness recipe

Description

A delicious recipe for Weakness, with Goldschlager® cinnamon schnapps, Rumple Minze® peppermint liqueur, Bacardi® 151 rum and Jagermeister® herbal liqueur.

Ingredients

1 oz Goldschlager® cinnamon schnapps

1 oz Rumple Minze® peppermint liqueur

1 oz Bacardi® 151 rum

1 oz Jagermeister® herbal liqueur

Instructions

Pour all four shots into a low ball glass, chill if you care.

Serving

Cocktail Glass

****

Westwood Ice Tea recipe

Description

A delicious recipe for Westwood Ice Tea, with Jose Cuervo® Especial gold tequila, Tanqueray® gin, Bacardi® light rum, Goldschlager® cinnamon schnapps, Bacardi® 151 rum and Stoli® Vanil vodka. Also lists simi

Ingredients

1 oz Jose Cuervo® Especial gold tequila

1 oz Tanqueray® gin

1 oz Bacardi® light rum

1 oz Goldschlager® cinnamon schnapps

3 splashes Bacardi® 151 rum

2 oz Stoli® Vanil vodka

Instructions

In a beer mug full of ice, pour in the tequila, gin, light rum and stir. Stir in the cinnamon schnapps, then stir in the vanilla vodka. Splash the high proof rum on top.

Serving

Beer Mug

****

Wet and Wild Lip Tickler recipe

Description

A delicious recipe for Wet and Wild Lip Tickler, with Bacardi® 151 rum, Midori® melon liqueur, creme de almond, triple sec and orange juice.

Ingredients

1/2 oz Bacardi® 151 rum

1 oz Midori® melon liqueur

1/2 oz creme de almond

1 oz triple sec

orange juice

Instructions

Pour ingredients as listed into an ice-filled collins glass. Garnish with an orange wedge, and serve.

Serving

Collins Glass
****

White Bat recipe

Description

A delicious recipe for White Bat, with Bacardi® white rum, Kahlua® coffee liqueur, milk and Coca-Cola®.

Ingredients

1 1/2 oz Bacardi® white rum
1/2 oz Kahlua® coffee liqueur
1 1/2 oz milk
3 oz Coca-Cola®

Instructions

Build all ingredients in a tall glass over ice. Stir, add a straw, and serve.

Serving

Highball Glass
****

White Mess recipe

Description

A delicious recipe for White Mess, with Bacardi® white rum, creme de cassis, root beer schnapps, Malibu® coconut rum and heavy cream.

Ingredients

1 part Bacardi® white rum
1 part creme de cassis
1 part root beer schnapps
1 part Malibu® coconut rum
1 part heavy cream

Instructions

In a mixing tin, combine all ingredients with ice and shake. Strain into a double shot glass. Can also be made tall (add a little soda water to cut down on the cream)

Serving

Shot Glass

****

Whitney recipe

Description

A delicious recipe for Whitney, with Bacardi® white rum, blush wine and lemon juice.

Ingredients

2 parts Bacardi® white rum
1 part blush wine
1 tbsp lemon juice

Instructions

Add ingredients chilled for better flavor. Avoid ice cubes to prevent watered down taste. Mix rum first (must be a white rum), add a dark type of wine (blush or red is fine), and finally a touch of lemon juice. Get ready to have fun!

Serving

Cocktail Glass
****

Wild Sex recipe

Description

A delicious recipe for Wild Sex, with Malibu® coconut rum, peach schnapps, Bacardi® 151 rum, orange juice, cranberry juice, pineapple juice and grenadine syrup.

Ingredients

1 oz Malibu® coconut rum
1/2 oz peach schnapps
1/2 oz Bacardi® 151 rum
1 oz orange juice
1 oz cranberry juice
1 oz pineapple juice
1/2 oz grenadine syrup

Instructions

Fill a hurricane glass with ice, pour in malibu, peach schnapps and 151. Pour juices on top followed by a splash of grenadine. Use a shaker tin to cover the glass and give a couple of good shakes.

Serving

Hurricane Glass
****

William Wallace recipe

Description

A delicious recipe for William Wallace, with Jose Cuervo® Especial gold tequila, Bacardi® 151 rum and Grey Goose® vodka.

Ingredients

1 oz Jose Cuervo® Especial gold tequila
1 oz Bacardi® 151 rum
1 oz Grey Goose® vodka

Instructions

Pour all three ingredients into a cocktail shaker half-filled with ice cubes. Shake well, strain into a large shot glass, and serve.

Serving

Shot Glass
****

Yellow Bird recipe

Description

A delicious recipe for Yellow Bird, with Bacardi® 151 rum, Galliano® herbal liqueur, vodka and sweet and sour mix.

Ingredients

1 oz Bacardi® 151 rum
1/2 oz Galliano® herbal liqueur
1/2 oz vodka
4 oz sweet and sour mix

Instructions

Pour all the alcoholic ingredients in a highball glass. Stir sour mix in a mixer and fill the glass.

Serving

Highball Glass
****

Yellow Parakeet recipe

Description

A delicious recipe for Yellow Parakeet, with Midori® melon liqueur, bananas, Bacardi® light rum, orange juice, pineapple juice and sweet and sour mix.

Ingredients

1 oz Midori® melon liqueur
1/2 oz bananas
1/2 oz Bacardi® light rum

2 counts orange juice
1 count pineapple juice
1 splash sweet and sour mix

Instructions

Fill glass with ice and build drink top with splash of sour.

Serving

Hurricane Glass
****

Zombie #6 recipe

Description

A delicious recipe for Zombie #6, with lemon juice, grenadine syrup, orange juice, cherry heering, Bacardi® white rum, Bacardi® black rum and 151 proof rum.

Ingredients

4 cl lemon juice
1 dash grenadine syrup
2 cl orange juice
2 cl cherry heering
2 cl Bacardi® white rum
6 cl Bacardi® black rum
2 cl 151 proof rum

Instructions

Mixed in a shaker on ice. Serve in a tumbler on crushed ice.

Serving

Old-Fashioned Glass
****

Zombie recipe

Description

A delicious recipe for Zombie, with Bacardi® 151 rum, pineapple juice, orange juice, apricot brandy, sugar, light rum, dark rum and lime juice.

Ingredients

1/2 oz Bacardi® 151 rum
1 oz pineapple juice
1 oz orange juice
1/2 oz apricot brandy
1 tsp sugar
2 oz light rum

1 oz dark rum
1 oz lime juice

Instructions

Blend all ingredients with ice except Bacardi 151 proof rum. Pour into a collins glass. Float Bacardi 151 proof rum on top. Garnish with a fruit slice, sprig of mint and a cherry.

Serving

COLLINS GLASS
****

Printed in Great Britain
by Amazon.co.uk, Ltd.,
Marston Gate.